City Finances, City Futures

John L. Mikesell
School of Public and Environmental Affairs
Indiana University

With comments from
John Petersen
Roy Bahl
Peter Harkness

**Challenge of a New Century:
The Future of America's Cities**

Michael A. Pagano and John K. Mahoney, Series Editors

336.014
M63c

The writing of and forum review for *City Finances, City Futures* was supported in part by the generous support of the George Gund Foundation.

 Text and cover printed on recycled paper.

Table of Contents

Foreword   The Challenge of a New Century:
The Future of America's Cities   i
by John P. Coleman and Donald J. Borut

Overview   vii

Introduction   1

Chapter 1   **People and Economic Activity in
Urban Areas**   3
Cities and Government Services   7

Chapter 2   **Fiscal Conditions in the
Intergovernmental Environment**   15
The Federal Deficit Overhang   15
States and Localities   19
Reorganization and Consolidation   23

Chapter 3   **City Revenue
Structure: Balancing Productivity,
Compassion, and Competition**   27
Current Revenue Patterns.   28
Traditional Property Taxes   32

	The Site Value Alternative	35
	Revenue Diversity	36
	Some Special Concerns	39
Chapter 4	**Cities, Infrastructure, and**	
	Bond Markets	**45**
	The Current City Debt Pattern	48
	Caught on the Level Playing Field	51
Chapter 5	**Consequences of City Fiscal Failure**	**53**
Chapter 6	**Positioning for the Future**	**57**
	Realism and City Leadership	57
	Revenue Diversity	59
	Self Reliance	60
	Conclusion	61
Notes		**63**
Comments		**69**
	Back to Basics	**71**
	John Petersen	
	Comparisons of Cities	72
	City Identity and Autonomy	73
	Fiscal Conditions and Intergovernmental	
	Environment	74
	Consolidation and Reorganization	76
	Privatization	77
	City Revenue Structures	78
	City Financial Failure	80
	Infrastructure, Bond Markets, and	
	Tax-Exemption	81
	Positioning For the Future	82

The Setting for City Finances in the 1990s   **85**

Roy Bahl

What Was Different About the 1980s?   86
What Are the Lessons From the 1980s?   88
What Do the 1990s Hold?   90

Cities on Their Own   **93**

Peter A. Harkness

Biographical Notes   **98**

Foreword

The Challenge of a New Century: The Future of America's Cities

About This Series

Since 1990, the Ohio Municipal League has been developing the ideas and resources for a series of forums on the future of America's cities. Within each forum, a first draft of the primary author's work, in this case John Mikesell's, is subjected to criticism from urban practitioners and observers and the revised for final publication. Each volume of the series is designed to include the primary work, as well as three of the many criticisms offered at the forum.

Because the focus of these works is national, the publication of this series is a joint effort of the Ohio League and the National League of Cities. Through this cooperation and the forum process, we hope to bring to readers studies that are a good merger of national and local, academic and practitioner insights into the future of the many aspects, challenges, and opportunities that face our nation's municipalities.

For many decades, municipal leagues in our nation have served as the legislative voices and practical education centers for the nation's cities, villages, and towns. Leagues, in many cases, also have served their member municipalities through a variety of direct services and technical assistance systems. The National League of Cities has served much the same purpose on the national level.

For the Ohio League and the National League of Cities, this process is one in which we ask some very old questions in a new way.

The "Challenge" series is an attempt to direct some of the Ohio League's energy, in cooperation with the National League of Cities, into an important activity that is as new to us as it is old to urban civilization. From Plato to Mumford and beyond, city-dwellers have taken the time to ask themselves about the nature and future of their communities. "What will our city be? What should our city be?" are questions that have echoed through thousands of years of urban civilization.

It is the underpinning belief of the "Challenge" series that much of the future of America's cities rests in how well we answer those questions. It is an underpinning hope of the series that, through it, we can bring some of America's best thinkers and practitioners together to answer some small pieces of those questions. More important, we hope this series will give the reader a good sense of the mosaic of questions that arise from those two simple inquiries for the late twentieth-century American city.

Foreword

In that sense, this series may contain more sparks for the reader's imagination than answers for the shelf. While this series contains a unity of focus, it is not designed to contain a unity of conclusions. This series is designed to give the reader a livelier curiosity about the challenges, the frustrations, and the overwhelming possibilities that urban lives and urban governments face over the next few decades. In that new curiosity, perhaps, you will, in your own way, help all of us answer those two simple questions a little better.

It is to encourage such contributions, from the authors and the readers of these volumes, that this series exists. The future of America's cities, like the development of all the world's cities, is not tied to one ideology, a few magic solutions, or the comings and goings of state and federal programs and policies. Throughout history, and in America today, cities have been the focus of society's capital, labor, culture, government, thought, and problems. Without cities, our nation would know neither great libraries nor race riots, neither great transportation systems nor shelters for the homeless.

Whether we like it or not, cities, large and small, will continue to serve as defining hubs of our civilization for decades to come. The attraction and aversion to all that is good and bad about cities of all shapes and sizes has been essential to the definition of our nation's development since, at least, the Civil War. Within that history, we have chosen cities and our reaction to cities as our primary medium for instituting change, organizing our lives, and giving a place to our hopes. Through the medium of cities, we have defined the domestic life of our nation.

Through this series' exploration of the future of that medium, we hope to see much of the future of our nation. That exploration could not be more timely. We believe we are now living in a time that will include the next great redefinition of the American city.

The last great redefinition, occurring in the wake of World War II, gave us the ascendancy of the suburban city and redefined everything from the length of our education to the size of our families. That redefinition gave us entirely new systems of transportation, communication, and entertainment. Within those changes, we saw the demise of the "big city machine" and the rise of the civil rights movement. The look, the problems, the opportunities, and the governance of our nation's cities changed dramatically during that period. Fired by different hopes, different values, and different technologies, the nation not only redefined the place of the central city in our lives, but also created a new diversity of city forms.

We now stand at the end of another great global conflict, the Cold War. Though that conflict affected us in ways different from past wars, we believe its conclusion may lead to the same kind of flurry of change that, as author Nicholas Lemann points out, has followed the other great conflicts in American history. Most of that change in this urban nation will be centered in our cities and will dramatically change the nature of those cities.

Certainly, this period of change will not mirror the last great redefinition of America's cities. The sweeping optimism embodied in such landmark efforts as the Interstate Highway System, the G.I. Bill, unprecedented assistance in building and buying homes, and tremendous growth in the affordability and availability of consumer goods that followed our nation's last great conflict does not seem present in our society today.

Foreword

Perhaps we are different. Certainly our challenges are different and our place in the world is different than it was four and
five decades ago. It may also be that we are within one of those
small moments in which we as a people reflect upon and begin
a major redefinition of our urban society. Encouraging that
reflection and developing our thoughts as a people about what
that new American city may be is the core and substance of
this series.

John P. Coleman	Donald J. Borut
Executive Director	Executive Director
Ohio Municipal League	National League of Cities

Volumes in this Series

Volume 1: A New Agenda for Cities: Richard P. Nathan
Volume 2: City Finances, City Futures: John Mikesell
Volume 3: Education and the Future of American Cities:
Richard F. Elmore
(1993)

City Finances, City Futures

Overview

This second volume of "The Challenge" series focuses on the future finance and taxation challenges that face our nation's municipalities. As such, it is a work that attempts to gauge the potential of several financial resources to provide or not provide the income for American urban services of the future. The breadth of such a discussion must stretch, as it does in this volume, from debt to taxes and fees to intergovernmental aid.

Though we will portray many aspects of the future American city in this series, perhaps none is more central to describing the future potential effectiveness of American municipal government than this fiscal picture drawn by John Mikesell.

The glue that binds political beliefs, philosophical visions, and unmet human needs with the day-to-day world of modern urban political life is fiscal. Cities in the past two decades have become painfully aware of the consequences of relying on federal and state beneficence, as federal aid diminishes or dries up and state aid is put on the chopping block during eras of fiscal retrenchment. As a consequence, cities are forced to become more reliant on their own revenue-generating capacity for purposes of financing their services than they have been for a long time. John Mikesell contends that the trend toward increasing self-reliance is not an aberration, that cities' future fiscal strength will rest on their own political and economic strengths, not on state or federal philanthropy.

According to studies by the U.S. Advisory Commission on Intergovernmental Relations, federal mandates on state and local governments have ballooned. Half of all mandates and preemption statutes ever enforced by the federal government since the founding of the Republic were imposed in the past quarter century. The effect on city finances is that cities increasingly are burdened by federal requirements and less able to meet their own needs. Moreover, Tenth Amendment protection has not been received well in the federal courts, as a series of cases has challenged the "juridical rights" of states and municipalities (especially the 1985 *Garcia* decision and the 1988 *South Carolina* case). In response to these sharp political changes, cities have continued to press their creators for greater revenue-raising autonomy and discretion.

Mikesell provides a glimpse into the future in which the federal watering hole is nearly dry, federal courts keep chipping away, and more and more issues are devolved to cities for resolution. Against this backdrop, the fiscal future of cities hinges on how much revenue-raising authority they're given, how creative they become in financing services, how adept they are at better targeting users of facilities and charging them for their use, and how competitive they are in expanding their tax bases. States can and will play a crucial role in encouraging or hindering cities' attempts to meet these challenges. These are the fiscal challenges for American cities not only for the remainder of this century, but more important, in the next century as well.

M.A.P.

J.K.M.

Introduction

Cities provide a locus for the economic, social, and cultural life of the nation. They provide government services critical to the human condition and to economic production, including those services vital for the safety and security of people and their property and for individual health, as well as amenities making life more pleasant. Large city governments often must provide public education. Thus, city governments supply critical services to their residents; more than half the nation's population lives in cities of more than ten thousand people. But city services are important for those living outside cities, because these people benefit when they commute to work in cities, visit them on pleasure or business, purchase the products of firms located in cities, or receive returns from city firms in which they have invested. Therefore, city governments, as providers of vital services, are critical for the economic life of the entire nation, even if one were to discount their unique importance as a cultural repository or architectural entity. If cities cannot deliver governmental services consistent with the reasonable demands of their residents, the whole nation must suffer.

Chapter 1

People and Economic Activity in Urban Areas

Urban areas in the United States provide advantages for economic and social activity. Population size and population density allow economies of scale in private manufacturing and other production and distribution functions. Concentrations of multiple economic functions and market density similarly play an important role. As an area grows, its population provides an enriched variety of labor supply capabilities available to many different producers, economic specialties develop, and the flow of the information important to economic and technological innovation becomes easier. As activity is concentrated, interurban transportation of people and property becomes more economical for entities near the urban concentration. In spite of economic and technological change, concentrations of people yield advantages in face-to-face communication, market density, and scale. Urban areas, if not cities themselves, retain special advantages in finance, communication, medicine, entertainment, culture, transportation, and government. Only basic agriculture and the extractive industries fail to follow that path—and the processing activities associated with these activities do tend toward concentration.

That pattern of economic advantage of urban areas produces a concentration of economic activity that benefits the persons living in those areas. An idea of its significance can be grasped from the data in **Table 1**, which compares per capita personal income in metropolitan areas and nonmetropolitan areas in each state in 1988. Although there are regional differences, the per capita personal income in metropolitan areas is 7.6 percent higher than the average for the state; the difference is smallest in the northeastern states and largest in the southern states. The same table also compares the per capita income in the county containing the largest city in each state with that of other areas. First, that county's per capita per-

---

Table 1. Comparing Per Capita Personal Incomes in Metropolitan and Non-Metropolitan Areas in Each Region, 1988.

	Nation	North east	North-Central	West	South
All Metropolitan Areas to All State	1.076	1.042	1.079	1.075	1.090
County of Largest City to All State	1.118	1.032	1.118	1.111	1.167
County of Largest City to All State Metropolitan Areas	1.038	0.989	1.036	1.034	1.068
County of Largest City to Its Metropolitan Area	1.008	0.955	1.022	1.000	1.032

Source: Computed from *Survey of Current Business*, April 1990. (Census region definitions used)

---

sonal income averages 11.8 percent higher than statewide per
capita income, again with least favorable advantage in the
northeast and largest in the south. Second, that county's per
capita income averages 3.8 percent higher than per capita
income in all state metropolitan areas, although not in the
northeastern states, where that county's income level is somewhat lower than for all metropolitan areas. The largest positive differential is in the south. Finally, the per capita income
of the county containing the largest city is only slightly greater
(0.8 percent) than that of its own metropolitan area. Again,
that county's level is about 5 percent lower than the metropolitan area level in the northeast and the advantage is
greatest in the southern states.

These data clearly show the greater relative economic affluence in metropolitan than nonmetropolitan areas of the nation. Differences are smaller in the northeast and greater in
the south. But these data reflect the economic advantages of
urban areas previously noted.

What about cities? Cities are the political subdivision found
normally in urban areas, with legal boundaries defined by
history or politics, often without great economic rationale.
They typically overlap other sub-state governments—counties, boroughs, parishes, special districts, and townships—
that are found through the state in both urban and nonurban
areas. Sometimes large city governments are combined with
their counties, sometimes cities are coterminous with their
overlapping county, and, in Virginia, cities are independent
of counties. As the form of local government that is particularly associated with urban areas, the city is the focus of
attention here. And that focus primarily is on the financing of
government services to people within that city.

City Finances, City Futures

Table 2 repeats the previous analysis, using the largest city in each state as the focus for per capita money income comparisons for 1985. Income estimates for 1985 are the most recent now available; analysis is done both for all states and for all states but those in which there is no geographic distinction between the largest city and an overlapping county. Several points are important to note. First, per capita money income in these largest cities typically is higher than in the state as a whole, about 5 percent higher across all states. The regional exception is the northeast, where city per capita money income is only around 85 percent of the state average.

Table 2. Comparing Per Capita Money Income Across Largest Cities in Each State, 1985.

Mean Ratios, All Fifty States

	Nation	North east	North-Central	West	South
Largest City to All State	1.051	0.864	1.056	1.125	1.076
County of Largest City to All State	1.101	1.011	1.123	1.099	1.131
Largest City to Its County	0.951	0.851	0.939	1.022	0.949

Means Ratios, Excluding States with Largest City Coterminous with County

	Nation	North east	North-Central	West	South
Largest City to All State	1.074	0.851	1.074	1.137	1.234
County of Largest City to All State	1.135	1.047	1.147	1.103	1.191
Largest City to its County	0.94	0.801	0.933	1.028	0.937

Source: U.S. Bureau of Census, *County and City Data Book 1988* (Washington: U.S. GPO, 1988). Regions are the same as in Table 1.

Second, these data, as did the prior ones, show the county containing the largest city to have higher per capita money income than the rest of the state. The difference is least for the northeast and greatest for the south. Finally, the comparisons show the largest city to have only about 95 percent of the per capita income of its surrounding county. In the west, it is slightly higher than the county level, but decidedly lower in the northeast.

These data are clear in their message. Per capita incomes in urban areas, and in large cities themselves, tend to be higher in urban areas than in the rest of the country. But per capita income in the large city is not as great as in the urban area surrounding the city. While there will certainly be exceptions, resources do concentrate in urban areas, but not necessarily in the largest cities of those areas. If those units face financial problems that cannot be managed from their own resources, the best avenue of access to additional financial resources is from the urban territories surrounding them. Relative affluence is more likely to be there than in the rest of the state. Indeed, one would be hard pressed to find a viable tax base for which per capita endowment in urban areas does not generally exceed that of the remainder of the state.[1]

Cities and Government Services

City governments provide particularly important services to persons and properties. **Table 3** and **Table 4** delineate these spending patterns, both in terms of defining the relative importance of city spending in the service category among all governments and the importance of the category in city spending. **Table 3** displays the relative importance of cities in spending by all American governments, thus outlining the extent of city responsibility for the service in the overlapping,

Table 3. The City Role in Provision of Government Services in the U.S., 1987-88.

Expenditure Category	City Share of Total Government Spending in Category
Total Direct General and Utility Expenditure	10.7
Total, less Defense, Space and Postal Expenditure	14.2
General Expenditure	
Education	5.5
Libraries	43.4
Public Welfare	4.7
Hospitals	11.3
Health	7.8
Highways	19.2
Air Transportation	26.3
Water Transportation	13.1
Police Protection	50.3
Fire Protection	69.9
Corrections	7.5
Protective Inspection and Regulation	26.4
Parks and Recreation	47.1
Housing and Community Development	26.0
Sewerage	59.4
Solid Waste Management	64.0
Government Administration	24.9
Interest on General Debt	4.9
Utility Expenditure	51.3
Water Supply	64.1
Electric Power	55.1
Gas Supply	79.7
Transit	25.1

Source: U.S. Bureau of Census, *Government Finances in 1987-1988*, GF-88-5.
(Washington: U.S. Government Printing Office, 1990.

multiservice federal system. **Table 4** portrays the importance of each service category in the finances of city government.

These data include both general expenditures and utility expenditures by the city government; compilations often segregate utility operations because governments may try to keep the utility services self-supporting through user charges and because legal restrictions may constrain the direct transfer of funds between general and utility operations. Furthermore, the utility category differs from other government services in the extent to which private providers regularly offer the service. Indeed, private firms provide water, electric power, gas supply, or transit service in many parts of the country without any government role (except regulation), city or otherwise. Even with that possibility, however, these services play an important role in overall city government service expenditure and are included here.[2]

In the context of all government expenditures, the data show an extraordinary city role (more than 40 percent of the total) in police protection, fire protection, parks and recreation, sewerage, solid waste management, libraries, water supply, electric power, and gas supply. Because electric power and gas supply, however, are more often privately than publicly provided in the United States, their relative significance in the compilation here exaggerates their true national importance. The special importance of city services in the intergovernmental context thus particularly centers on protection of persons and property (police and fire protection), managing waste created by society (sewerage and solid waste management), distribution of water, and important amenities for life (libraries and parks and recreation). Cities also have significant shares of other important service categories, including hospitals, highways, air and water transportation, protective inspection and regulation, housing and community development (as with utilities, private provision plays an important role here), and transit. But cities overall play a smaller role in education (primary, secondary, and higher), public welfare, and health,—all categories of great importance to city residents. These functions, in the American assignment of responsibilities, are the tasks of other governments, some-

Table 4. Significance of Expenditure Categories by City Size Group (1986 population): Percentage of City Direct General and Utility Expenditure in Expenditure Category: 1987-88.

Category	All cities	1,000,000 or more	500,000 to 999,000	300,000 to 499,000
Direct General	79.5%	85.5%	80.3%	80.7%
Education	8.7	12.6	9.5	6.3
Libraries	1.0	0.9	0.8	1.0
Public Welfare	3.9	11.1	5.1	0.5
Hospitals	3.5	5.3	4.2	1.7
Health	1.3	1.8	2.6	1.6
Highways	6.4	3.2	5.0	5.4
Air Transportation	1.5	1.9	2.9	3.2
Police Protection	9.3	7.9	8.3	9.7
Fire Protection	4.9	3.2	4.4	6.0
Corrections	1.0	2.2	2.2	0.8
Protective inspection and Regulation	0.7	0.6	0.7	0.8
Parks and Recreation	3.8	2.3	3.7	5.7
Housing & Community Development	3.9	5.6	3.8	4.2
Sewerage	6.0	4.3	5.9	7.2
Solid Waste Management	2.8	2.6	2.0	3.0
Government Administration	5.7	3.9	5.7	5.2
Interest on General Debt	5.9	4.4	6.3	9.4
Utilities	20.5	14.5	19.7	19.3
Water Supply	7.2			
Electric Power	9.6			
Gas Supply	1.4			
Transit	2.4			

Source: U.S. Bureau of Census, *City Government Finances in 1987-88*. Categories will not add to 100 percent because of rounding and omitted small groups.

times state, but often overlapping counties and single-purpose
districts that are politically and fiscally independent from,
although sometimes having boundaries that match the city.

Table 4 examines the spending patterns of cities across
categories, in total and by population size group. The division
is remarkable for the fact that few categories represent as
much as ten percent of total city expenditure. Significant
expenditure categories are police and fire protection, educa-

**Table 4. Significance of Expenditure Categories by City
Size Group (1986 population): Percentage of City Direct
General and Utility Expenditure in Expenditure Category:
1987-88.**

Category	200,000 to 299,000	100,000 to 199,000	75,000 to 99,000	Less than 75,000
Direct General	83.2%	77.9%	83.0%	74.1%
Education	13.1	11.4	11.5	4.3
Libraries	1.1	1.2	1.2	1.0
Public Welfare	1.0	1.1	0.5	0.4
Hospitals	2.1	2.0	2.1	3.0
Health	3.1	1.0	0.7	0.4
Highways	6.4	7.0	8.2	9.1
Air Transportation	1.2	1.7	0.6	0.4
Police Protection	8.6	9.4	10.7	10.6
Fire Protection	5.6	6.4	6.7	5.4
Corrections	0.3	0.3	0.0	0.0
Protective inspection and Regulation	0.9	0.8	1.1	0.8
Parks and Recreation	5.7	4.3	5.4	4.1
Housing & Community Development	4.5	3.4	4.2	2.6
Sewerage	4.9	5.5	5.3	7.4
Solid Waste Management	3.0	2.7	2.5	3.2
Government Administration	5.0	5.6	6.2	7.2
Interest on General Debt	8.4	5.3	7.2	5.9
Utilities	16.8	22.1	17.0	25.9

tion, sewerage, highways, and utilities. For any city, of course, the assignment of functions in the state-local relationship in which it operates may differ from these general patterns. For instance, cities that have dependent school systems (schools managed as an operation of city government, rather than as a part of an independent school district) would require higher shares of their budgets for education; dependent school systems operate in such major cities as New York, Buffalo, Boston, Baltimore, Hartford, and Richmond. Similarly, there are differences by city size, notably in spending for public welfare, highways, police protection and corrections.

While the patterns of responsibility and, therefore, the service expectations vary across states and by city size, the system of government finances has left cities with critical service assignments. Some shedding of responsibility to other levels or to special districts may occur, especially for functions like education, highways, public welfare, transit, or sewerage-solid waste management, where demands are likely to be high and service impacts have significant implications beyond city boundaries. But the era of service shedding and realignment of responsibility is as likely to be behind cities as it is to be ahead of them and, where realignment occurs, it may not create greatly increased flexibility. One examination of the establishment of special districts notes that such districts are created "without the approval of existing cities and countries in the area. This can erode the general-purpose governments' unique capacity for setting priorities in meeting the multiple needs in each area and for coordinating the provision of services effectively and efficiently."[3]

Service shedding and realignment of responsibility can be reasonable when needs of the population being served are wider than the city.[4] But with the change in responsibility from the city to another government will ordinarily come a loss of city control over delivery of that service. Any new fiscal flexibility gained by shedding the responsibility would be no bargain if the city population faces a problem that the new district cannot or will not resolve. Furthermore, new districts will draw from the same underlying economic base as the city, creating a strong possibility of fiscal competition with the city. New districts to handle service responsibilities offer no general answer to city fiscal dilemmas, even when cities play a significant role in their governance. They can, however, contribute in the overall matrix of service delivery within cities.

Chapter 2

Fiscal Conditions in the Intergovernmental Environment

Cities operate in a multi-level federal system. Because they have received considerable resources from their partner governments, and because some traditional city functions have been realigned to other units, some attention needs to be given financial prospects elsewhere in the federal system. It should be recognized that, in 1987-88, municipal governments received 5.4 percent of their general revenue from the federal government, 20.7 percent from state government, and 2.3 percent from local governments.[5] How are prospects for the future?

The Federal Deficit Overhang

The persistent federal deficit presently constrains federal capacity to participate aggressively in new initiatives. In each fiscal year since 1969, the federal government has spent more than it has received. While that record might be taken as evidence that federal deficits are unimportant, there is at least political evidence to the contrary. Politicians fear that deterioration in American international competitiveness may stem from inadequate private investment induced by the drain of capital to finance the deficit. They fear a run-up of domestic interest rates, should foreign holders of treasury debt start unloading the portfolios they accumulated over the past two decades. They fear the share of federal spending that debt service must take and the need to constrain other initiatives that might use federal resources. And, possibly most of all, they sense a public unease with a government that seems unable to manage its finances as well as ordinary households must.

The impact of these fears has been a series of federal deficit control laws, each intended to be so Draconian as to induce deficit constraint and eventual budget balance. **Figure 1** shows the influence after 1985 of such measures until budget participants learned ways around the control system. The progress shown after 1990 reflects estimates and hopes. But it does emphasize the attitude that deficits need to be controlled. Lawrence Haas summarizes: "Only by fixing the deficit problem can policy makers return to the period of powerful government. But their short-term interests may not allow such a fix."[6] Neither spending reductions nor revenue increases have much political attractiveness. Perversely enough, the federal government is not likely to become a powerful participant until it finds a way to correct the imbalance and the accompanying perception that the United States government is somehow impoverished.

What implications does this prospect hold for cities? In general, cities should not expect major increases in federal aid will soon arrive. Congress, facing pressure for fiscal conservatism, is unlikely to endure politically wrenching choices among federal programs and to contemplate the difficult question of raising additional revenue, only to allow another level of government to spend those resources. The federal budget for 1992 reflects prospects for future federal aid (**Table 5**) that reflect a continuation of historic trends in assistance. Intergovernmental aid—not aid to individuals—peaked in real terms in 1978. Its descent has been essentially uninterrupted since then, and that path appears in plans through 1996. The reduction has been less for capital investment (especially as supported by the Transportation trust funds) than for other aid. It would be hazardous to expect federal aid to assume an increased role in city finances; declines are much more likely.[7]

Figure 1. Federal Budget Deficit in Relation to Gross National Product (including social insurance)

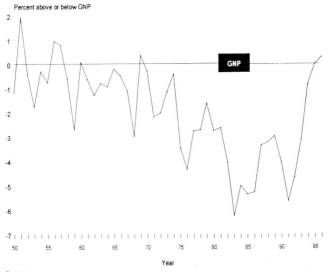

Source:
U.S. Office of Management and Budget, *Budget of the United States Government, Fiscal Year 1992*

Although direct aid to cities is not highly probable, there are
some prospects for relief. Congress is more likely to provide
assistance to individuals living in cities than to cities themselves. It is consistent with the political imperative that those
responsible for raising the funds receive the accolades for
spending those funds. Such a profile does appear in **Table 5**.
If federal resources remain constrained, any use of those
resources will need to be clearly labeled as "courtesy of Congress." Federal aid is more likely to flow to people, not places,
but help with individual poverty, homelessness, substance
abuse, health, and so on will ultimately help the places in

**Table 5. Federal Aid to Individuals and State and Local
Governments, 1977-1996.**

| | Aid in Billions of 1982 Dollars | | | | Percent of Total Aid | | |
Fiscal Year	Total	To Individuals	For Capital Investment	Other State and Local Aid	To Individuals	For Capital Investment	Other Aid
1977	$103.6	$34.2	$24.8	$44.7	33.0%	23.9%	43.1%
1978	109.7	34.9	25.7	49.2	31.8%	23.4%	44.8%
1979	106.6	35.7	24.7	46.3	33.5%	23.2%	43.4%
1980	105.9	38.2	24.5	43.2	36.1%	23.1%	40.8%
1981	100.7	40.3	22.7	37.7	40.0%	22.5%	37.4%
1982	88.2	38.8	20.1	29.3	44.0%	22.8%	33.2%
1983	88.8	40.8	20.3	27.7	45.9%	22.9%	31.2%
1984	90.2	41.8	21.9	26.5	46.3%	24.3%	29.4%
1985	94.1	44.0	22.9	27.1	46.8%	24.3%	28.8%
1986	97.1	47.1	23.6	26.4	48.5%	24.3%	27.2%
1987	90.8	48.3	21.1	21.3	53.2%	23.2%	23.5%
1988	92.7	50.1	21.1	21.5	54.0%	22.8%	23.2%
1989	93.7	51.8	20.3	21.7	55.3%	21.7%	23.2%
1990	100.9	57.8	20.9	22.2	57.3%	20.7%	22.0%
1991 est.	110.4	65.8	20.7	24.0	59.6%	18.8%	21.7%
1992 est.	113.9	70.9	19.8	23.2	62.2%	17.4%	20.4%
1993 est.	117.8	75.7	20.0	22.2	64.3%	17.0%	18.8%
1994 est.	121.4	80.9	19.4	21.1	66.6%	16.0%	17.4%
1995 est.	124.7	85.7	18.6	20.3	68.7%	14.9%	16.3%
1996 est.	128.0	89.9	18.6	19.5	70.2%	14.5%	15.2%

Source: *Budget of The United States Government, Fiscal Year 1992*, p. 7-132.

which those individuals live. There is also some possibility of assistance in the management of environmental problems. The flow of pollutants across city and state borders begs for national intervention. Although the action could entail regulation without resources, there is a reasonable chance that earmarked charges and fees could be translated into help for governments assigned mitigation responsibilities, including cities. Specific districts covering larger areas may be formed to deal with some environmental problems, again providing cities some relief.

States and Localities

State and local governments face a different budget constraint than does the federal government. While the federal government enjoys the ultimate financing option of creating money, thereby allowing its debt to be the international benchmark for security of principal, state and local governments must always watch the quality and marketability of their debt: "The bottom line in fiscal discipline is the credit market...[A state or locality] must either pay for its expenditures and bonded indebtedness in a timely manner or face limited and expensive terms in the credit markets."[8] These governments are thus regulated by credit markets to an extent not felt by the federal government. They simply do not have the ultimate backstop of money creation. State and local governments must observe the judgment of credit markets in their budget structures.

The market discipline, regardless of any legal strictures, means that state and local governments, both individually and in the aggregate, will be keen to restrain their deficits. These governments will not balance their aggregate expenditure and revenue each year; most will borrow to finance capital spending. But the discipline of the credit market prevents an unchecked imbalance.

Figure 2 reports the combined state and local surplus or deficit as a percentage of gross national product for the past twenty years. These data exclude the operations of associated social insurance funds (state and local employee retirement, temporary disability insurance, and workers' compensation). Unlike similar federal funds, state and local governments lack easy access to these resources to finance general deficits, either by easy loans or direct subsidization. These surpluses and deficits thus include general, utility, and liquor store operations of state and local government, the sectors responsible for delivery and finance of services to the public. Over these years, significant movements toward deficits have usually been associated with national recessions (1969-70, 1973-75, 1980, 1981-82).[9] However, the worsening combined

Figure 2. Combined State and Local Government Surplus or Deficit in Relation to Gross National Product, 1970-1990 (excluding social insurance)

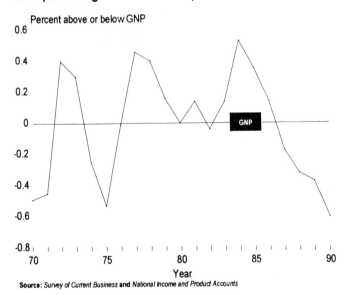

Percent above or below GNP

Source: *Survey of Current Business* **and** *National Income and Product Accounts*

surplus (and eventual deficit) starting in 1985 was not associated with recession. This poses fundamental fiscal questions for the state-local sector of which cities are a part.

Does this recent pattern mean that the state-local sector will be unable to accommodate public demands for services? There is reason for long term optimism. First, the credit market corrective will work. Resolution will entail combinations of spending and revenue adjustments, but that is not an unrealistic requirement, and it is one that state and local governments have historically been able to handle. Second, some considerable amount of recent deficit increases undoubtedly involves a leading response of fiscal systems to the 1990-91 national recession. As the economy recovers, the deficits are likely to decline and return to surplus. Third, the recent deficits are swamped by the levels of state and local government expenditure on structures, notably for highways, water supply facilities, and buildings for education.[10] Use of credit for such spending can spread the cost of long-life facilities over their useful life and is consistent with prudent fiscal management. And finally, while recent deficits in the state and local sector have been huge in absolute terms, their relative size is smaller than experienced in the 1950-1970 period: the 1970-1990 mean deficit is 0.02 percent of gross national product, compared with 0.53 percent for the earlier period.

These data obviously provide no direct basis for easier fiscal relations between the state and local government sector and cities for the future. But they do suggest a capacity to balance local budgets generally absent from federal government. There is more hope for a supportive financial relationship for cities from the state government than from the federal government. **Figure 3** traces the path of federal and state aid to cities since 1973. It shows both the decline in the federal role starting in the late 1970s and the gradual recovery of state aid to cities that began in the late 1980s. The pattern now in place is more consistent with the traditional federal relationship. More state aid is both likely and consistent with tradition.

Figure 3. Federal and State Aid to Cities as a Share of City General Revenue, 1973-1988

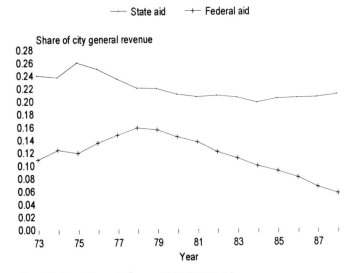

Source: U.S. Bureau of Census, *City Government Finances* (various years)

In the American governmental system, cities are created by their states. Judge John F. Dillon identified the relationship more than a century ago: "Municipal corporations owe their origin to, and derive their powers and rights wholly from, the legislature. It breathes into them the breath of life, without which they cannot exist. As it creates, so it may destroy. If it may destroy, it may abridge and control."[11] That fundamental relationship between a state and its cities reminds us that state government reserves ultimate control. If things go horribly wrong in the city, those dependent on it can expect the state to intervene; this has been the experience in New York, Pennsylvania, and elsewhere. No such fundamental link between the federal government and cities exists, despite the undeniable importance of cities to the life of the nation.

Reorganization and Consolidation

Local governments, including cities, have identities of their own. People live in particular places because the mix of private and public circumstances there meet their preferences better than do other options open to them. City government provides a major component of how one place differs from another, including both the level, quality, and variety of public services provided and the manner in which those services are financed. City *autonomy* and *independence* provide the foundation for the *identity* that defines the essence of the city.

Government consolidation conflicts with the principle of identity. Unification of separate cities reduces the amount of governmental diversity available to individuals and businesses; it is almost certain to make part of the unified combination feel left out of the process; and it will likely generate fiscal tensions as some areas feel certain that they are unfairly subsidizing the wasteful behavior of others. Wounds can last for years.[12]

Similar tensions accompany city-county consolidations. The residents of cities and surrounding unincorporated areas often have different ideas about and needs for local public services. A dual system of local governments provides for those differences and allows greater individual choice. Until a city actually grows to encompass the geographic extent of a county, governmental combinations will destroy identities and thwart legitimate desires for different local government services. When some city concerns extend beyond its political bounds, special districts can be more consistent with the needs of government identity and city preference than are general purpose government combinations. Indeed, one widely-noted combined government, the Indianapolis-Marion County (Indiana) Unigov, can best be described as a partially overlapping series of special districts with interior independent cities than as a completely consolidated government.

But what about economies of scale from a larger size government? Consolidation and combination would lower unit cost to make taxpayers better off. There are two important problems with this argument. First, the empirical evidence shows that, with the exception of certain services with capital intensive production, particularly water, sewer, electric, and gas, economies of scale do not exist. Traditional local government services, like police and fire protection, operate with unit costs that do not vary over a wide range of operating scale.[13] Thus, there would be no unit cost advantage associated with consolidating or combining; simply a loss of local identity, autonomy, and control.

Second, any economies of scale, to the extent they exist, apply to conditions of production only and do not prescribe the size of the government needed to make choices about provision or financing. A government too small to produce a particular service most economically may arrange to buy that service from a larger private, non-profit, or government producer. We do not expect households to be large enough to produce inexpensive automobiles if they want to purchase a car; similar principles apply to choices about city government size.

Another element of city reorganization deals with the possibility of privatization. The term has been stretched to cover many structural changes and, accordingly, has suffered enor-

mously. In the context of contracting out, the service continues
to be publicly provided when a governmental body decides
whether to have the service, at what quality and quantity,
who the producer will be, and how the service will be financed
(by current or future revenues, by taxes or charges, etc.).[14]
Production—including the operating, delivering, and managing—of the service is the responsibility of the other party to
the contract. In this context, privatization is reasonable; the
cost of supplying the desired quantity and quality of service
should be the driving factor in the choice between private or
public production. Provision of the service remains public.

The other extreme of privatization, however, envisions an end
to public involvement, getting government out of its role as
provider, regulator, or decision maker. Households and businesses would then assume the role of service provider, if the
service is to be provided at all. When the service is market-
able—in other words, when the buyer of a service can obtain
full rights to the service being purchased, without considerable benefits being enjoyed by those who have not paid—private provision works well and government load-shedding is
entirely reasonable. But many local services are not market-
able, or they have accompanying expectations that they will
benefit disadvantaged individuals. In that context, privatization represents a cruel hoax and disservice to the public. It
cannot be viewed as a general response to tight city finances
in either context.

Chapter 3

City Revenue Structure: Balancing Productivity, Compassion, and Competition

Cities operate in the revenue context of the federal system. Their most important legal constraints are those their states place on them to prohibit or confine city revenue actions. States typically determine which tax and user charge options are available to their cities. They often limit the rates that may be levied on those bases or the revenues that may be collected from them, and they may prescribe the manner in which the tax or charge may be collected. States also collect revenue from most of these same sources, and they sometimes provide cities cooperative administration, often at no cost to the city. Cities also draw directly on the same economic base as overlapping local governments (counties, schools, other single purpose districts, and others) and important city taxes are often administered by other local units. Furthermore, as the largest single draw on the total revenue base, the operations of the federal government provide a critical backdrop for city revenue operations. The city revenue environment includes competing claimants, options precluded by actions of superior governments, and opportunities provided by other units. The revenue structure finally chosen by a city, along with the services it provides, defines what that government is for its residents and for others.

Current Revenue Patterns.

Local governments in the United States have had a remarkable dependence on property taxation as a source for the revenue they raise, 40.1 percent of own-source revenue (including utilities) and 74.1 percent of tax revenue in 1987-88.[15] In part, it is remarkable because of regular array of charges against the tax and predictions of its demise. One of the most widely-cited forecasts was by George Mitchell in a 1956 address to the National Tax Association that, in twenty years, "the property tax will... have become an all-but-forgotten relic of an earlier fiscal age."[16] That forecast has not come true. Indeed, the 1980s brought a slowdown in the movement of local revenue systems away from the property tax: the property tax share of local general revenue was 2.4 percentage points lower in 1960 than in 1950, 7.1 points lower in 1970 than in 1960, 12.5 points lower in 1980 than in 1970, but 1.1 points higher in 1988 than in 1980.[17] Despite its weaknesses, the property tax is productive, generally reliable in difficult economic times, and adaptable to a complex geography of overlapping local governments.

The city government revenue profile is more diverse and less property-tax-reliant than are local governments in aggregate, however. **Table 6** portrays the current city role in the overall state and local government structure and presents the distribution of city revenue among the several categories of flow.

Table 6. The City Role in the State-Local Revenue System in the U.S.

Revenue Category	City Share of All State-Local Revenue in Category, 1987-88	Significance of Category in All City Own Source Revenue 1987-88	1971-72
Own Source Revenue (General plus Utility)	19.4%	100.0%	100.0%
Own Source			
General Revenue	16.0	76.3	80.1
Taxes	13.7	46.8	58.0
Property	22.6	23.5	37.3
General Sales and Gross Receipts	9.7	8.0	6.4
Selective Sales and Gross Receipts	12.8	5.1	4.5
Motor Fuel	1.4	0.2	0.1
Alcoholic Beverage	5.5	0.2	0.2
Tobacco	2.8	0.1	0.5
Public Utility	36.8	3.0	2.6
Other	14.4	1.6	1.1
Individual Income	7.2	5.0	}6.4
Corporate Income	8.7	1.6	
Licenses	1.7	0.2	}3.4
Other	25.5	3.5	
Current Charges	22.6	16.7	13.3
Hospitals	13.6	2.8	2.9
Airports	43.5	1.4	1.1
Park & Recreation	44.4	1.1	0.8
Housing and Community Development	40.3	0.8	0.9
Sewerage	67.1	5.3	3.1
Solid Waste Management	62.1	1.6	1.1
Other	10.6	3.8	3.5
Miscellaneous Revenue	20.5	12.7	8.7
Interest earnings	20.0	7.4	2.3
Other	21.1	5.3	6.3
Utility Revenue	61.5	23.7	19.9
Electric Power	59.0	12.1	7.6
Water Supply	68.1	8.2	8.7
Transit	36.9	1.4	2.6
Gas Supply	79.6	1.8	1.0

Source: U.S. Bureau of Census, *Government Finances in 1987-1988*, GF-88-5 (Washington: U.S. Government Printing Office, 1990); U.S. Bureau of Census, *City Government Finances: 1987-88*, GF-88-4 (Washington: U.S. Government Printing Office, 1990); and U.S. Bureau of Census, *Census of Governments, 1972. Vol. 4. Government Finances, No. 4. Finances of Municipalities and Township Governments* (Washington: U.S. Government Printing Office, 1974)

Because cities function in a system of local governments created by their states, their share in that combined system is critical. The federal revenue structure is not included here; the federal government relies so heavily on the income taxes, despite its recent renewed incursions into selective excise taxation, that its inclusion would swamp that category with little of importance to be found among other classes.

In the combined state-local revenue system, the city share is large for categories involving direct user payment. More than 40 percent of all state and local government collections generated by airports, parks and recreation activities, housing, sewerage, solid waste management, electric power, water supply, and gas supply are from city governments. Cities are important government sellers of services in those areas.[18] Only in the public utility excise tax classification is there even approximately as great a city share of tax collections. Thus, cities dominate several important charge categories, revenue classes where the government might be expected to behave more like a private business than a government; they do not dominate important tax categories. They do, however, collect more than twenty percent of American property taxes.

Table 7 shows the patterns of revenue reliance for all cities and across several size classes. The distributions show that the smaller cities rely more heavily on utility revenue than do the largest cities, that the largest cities (populations greater than 500,000) rely more heavily (dramatically so) on the income tax than do other cities, and that cities with populations over one million rely more heavily on the general sales tax than do other cities, although the difference is much less extreme than for the income tax. The larger cities show greater tax diversity than the smaller ones: more than 60 percent of the tax revenue in the group of cities with population over one million comes from taxes other than property

Table 7. Significance of Revenue Categories by City Size Group (1986 population): Percentages of Own Source General and Utility Revenue: 1987-88

Category	All Cities	1,000,000 or more	500,000 to 999,000	3000,000 to 499,000	2000,000 to 299,000	100,000 to 199,000	75,000 to 99,000	Less than 75,000
General Revenue	76.3	84.6	78.1	80.1	78.8	72.2	79.7	69.9
Taxes	46.8	61.9	49.8	43.3	43.5	43.0	48.2	38.2
Property	23.5	24.0	24.2	19.8	21.4	26.5	30.5	22.3
General Sales	8.0	9.9	7.0	8.8	8.7	6.9	9.2	6.8
Selective Sales	5.1	7.0	5.0	6.2	6.0	4.8	4.2	3.
Income	6.6	16.3	9.5	4.6	4.0	1.6	0.9	2.2
Other	3.7	4.7	4.1	4.0	3.3	3.2	3.3	3.1
Current Charges	16.7	13.9	16.1	19.6	20.3	17.0	17.1	17.
Miscellaneous	12.7	8.0	12.2	17.3	15.1	12.2	14.4	14.
Utility Revenue	23.7	15.4	21.9	19.9	21.2	27.8	20.3	30.

Source: U.S. Bureau of Census, *City Government Finances : 1987-88*, GF-88-4 (Washington: U.S. Government Printing Office, 1990).

taxes. This holds true for more than 50 percent for the groups through the 200,000 population range. Property tax reliance is greater—around 60 percent or more—for the smaller cities.

City governments rely on taxes, which is certainly not remarkable for general purpose governments; among the taxes, reliance is greatest on the property tax. That reliance is, however, less than for other general purpose local governments (counties and townships). In 1987-88, these other localities raised 61.4 percent of own-source revenue from taxes, a considerably larger proportion than the 46.8 percent for cities. Property taxes constitute 76.6 percent of tax revenue for those units, compared with 50.2 percent for cities.[19] The property tax share for school districts is dramatically higher. In that local government context, city governments have considerable revenue diversity, particularly in the use of general and selective sales taxes, income taxes, and charges received by utilities and collected by government operations.

While the pattern of diversity, particularly with regard to taxes used, has changed little in the past decade, there has been greater realignment in comparison with the early 1970s. Cities rely less on the property tax and more on general and selective sales taxes, on income taxes, on charges, and on utilities. These changes are likely to continue for the foreseeable future. But it would be folly to predict replacement of the property tax. In spite of its many flaws, the ability to produce revenue counts. In that respect, the property tax has a proven record over the history of American cities.

Traditional Property Taxes

In his 1931 classic treatise on property taxation, Jensen wrote: "If any tax could have been eliminated by adverse criticism, the general property tax should have been eliminated long ago..."[20] Just as they did more than half a century ago, property tax critics have an extensive bill of indictments.

First, assessment quality is abysmal. Values assigned property parcels usually fall below the levels that fair application of the legal assessment standard would imply and, more importantly for equitable treatment of taxpayers, the ratio of assessed value to the legal standard (often market value) varies dramatically from one property to another. That variation assures that similar properties, subject to exactly the same property tax rates, will pay dramatically different property taxes. The most recent national study of assessment quality found good assessment quality in only twelve percent of the 1,367 areas surveyed.[21] Because the property tax, unlike sales or income taxes, requires estimation of a stock value, not an annual tally of transactions, the tax has special administrative problems. Few governments assign resources commensurate to the task, so abysmal quality is to be expected, in spite of significant effort by many tax assessors. While there is a dispute about whether the property tax creates vertically inequitable (regressive) burden patterns,[22] there is absolutely no dispute that, as administered, the tax produces non-uniformity in tax burdens.

A second property tax problem is the extent to which the tax, as commonly implemented, can discourage economic development and redevelopment, and even help transmit urban blight. Property taxes, applied to actual use of land and improvements on that land, will ordinarily increase when a holder develops, redevelops, or renovates a property. Critics argue that this property tax wedge can tip decisions against such investment, much to the detriment of the local economy. Furthermore, the system of enforcement against delinquent property—infrequent property sales for back taxes—can work as a transmitter of urban blight. The subject property, in limbo either because a tax sale purchaser does not receive immediate title or because no prospective purchaser has bid an amount sufficient to cover delinquent taxes, can become derelict, a magnet for vagrants and illicit activity and a transmitter of decline to surrounding properties. Thus. the tax may discourage economic development and accelerate decline in weakened neighborhoods.

And third, the property tax, as a tax on accumulated value and not on a transaction value, can place extraordinary distress through surprisingly high property tax bills as development occurs. Special attention is given the plight of the elderly: suppose the family homestead, a property appropriate to the needs of a growing family and entirely affordable on the household's income, happens to be in an economically developing area. The market value of the property jumps, as does the value for property tax purposes, and the tax on the property increases beyond the normal means of the homeowners, now living on retirement funds, to afford. The increased property value, the basis for the tax increase, is accessible only if the property holders sell, which they do not wish to do.[23] The family must choose between crippling property tax bills or sale of the homestead. Similar jumps in assessed value, although not always producing higher tax bills, accompany periodic mass reassessments conducted to realign tax values to legal standards. In general, tax values may increase dramatically without easily apparent means of paying the accompanying tax.

But property taxes continue as an important city revenue source. How have they survived?

First, property tax revenue is substantial and would be difficult to replace without dramatic increases in the rates applied to other bases. Heavy use of these alternative sources could make their impacts untenable.

Second, the property tax produces cyclically stable revenue. Except for the experience of national depression, property tax collections flow without significant disruption through business cycles.[24] For jurisdictions, like cities, that lack easy access to credit markets, that reliability is an important advantage.

Third, property taxes, especially those on real property, are not clearly an inappropriate basis for dividing the cost of supporting many local services, particularly those which directly benefit the holders of the property. Furthermore, while the connection between property holding and actual affluence is less strong than it was at earlier times of American history, property value, particularly for homeowners, is an index of capacity to bear the cost of government.

And finally, the manner of real property administration does allow great geographic variation in rates, reflecting different service and taxing districts, a variation probably not feasible with any other tax base.

Governments are better able to administer the real property tax than they have ever been before. Geographic information systems allow mapping, integration of multi-faceted data flows, and information access never previously possible. Information on property transactions is almost globally accessible and would become even better with new Internal Revenue Service reporting requirements. The discipline and technology of assessment and appraisal have developed to a level not expected in prior eras. But the public does not like the property tax, and governments are not apt to devote to its administration the resources necessary for its proper operation. Cities, because they tend not to do the property valuation, are trapped by the poor quality of administration done by others. Overall, the property tax contribution to city finances is not likely to increase substantially in the future.

The Site Value Alternative

Site value taxation has long been proposed as an alternate to the traditional property tax in urban areas. This restructuring would apply tax to land value but would exclude (or tax lightly) the value of improvements. The exclusion would remove an important disincentive for development, rehabilitation, and economic growth; the tax bill would be determined according to the value that could be earned from the most valued use of the particular site. No allowance would be made for the current use of the site and development on the site would have no impact on its taxable value.

The concept derives from the ideas of Henry George from slightly more than a century ago. A tax on land has fewer efficiency distortions than other taxes because land is in fixed supply. Taxing land according to its highest yield will induce holders to bring parcels to that use. Furthermore, the tax is regarded as especially equitable: high land values largely result from social progress—development of roads, schools, and airports, for example—and thus are largely *unearned* by the holder. That makes returns from landholding particularly legitimate targets for taxation. Current applications are mostly in other countries, although some Pennsylvania cities use some principles of site value tax structures.[25] If cities can obtain the authority to experiment, can get acceptance for removing the tax on urban structural improvements, and will devote sufficient resources to site value assessment, such a tax should be helpful reform for urban finances.

Revenue Diversity

The property tax will not disappear from city revenue systems, but income taxes, sales taxes, and prices paid by city service customers will take on a more important role in these fiscal systems. Because most states levy general sales and individual income taxes, such city taxes could be cooperatively administered. That would reduce taxpayer compliance confusion and would almost certainly improve the overall quality of administering the taxes. Few but the largest cities could mount audit and enforcement programs comparable to those of their states. And, for income taxes, states do base their taxes on more inclusive income concepts patterned after the federal systems. A number of cities limit their taxes to payroll, thus omitting incomes (such as interest, dividends, and capital gains) of relatively greater significance to the more affluent. Using the more inclusive base thus improves the prospects for fairness in the tax burden. Piggybacking involves loss of a city option on the design of the tax base. Improved compliance and breadth generally make the loss worthwhile. Piggybacked administration currently is the rule for local sales taxation, but remains the exception for local income taxation.

City income and sales taxes can have adverse impacts on the city economy and revenue flows, for the taxes do not always accrue to the units with greatest fiscal need. A number of states have mitigated these problems by requiring adoption by a geographically broader unit, usually a county, with revenues distributed among cities and other entities in the adopting area by pre-arranged formula. While such a system forecloses individual choice of statutory rates within the adopting area and probably requires state administration, its fiscal and economic advantages outweigh those limitations. The city gains an important new element for its revenue base, with minimal loss of fiscal flexibility and autonomy.

Greater use of sales revenue, or financing through voluntary exchange, can never supplant taxes, or financing by coercion, in the city revenue portfolio. Indeed, as Alice Rivlin has pointed out, "User fees have always appealed more to economists than to politicians."[26] And the objection is not solely political. Many city services intend to provide special benefits to less affluent members of the population; many services accrue generally to the populace and significant benefits would be provided non-purchasers, should any person choose to pay; and many services, while yielding benefits to clearly defined persons, could be restricted to purchasers only at considerable expense. So there are important limits to city revenue diversification to prices from taxes.

In service areas where the beneficiary is clear-cut, where the beneficiary can truly be given a choice of purchasing the service or declining, and where the cost of collecting the price is not prohibitive, greater use of direct prices would be appropriate. That strategy prevents those using the service from receiving special subsidization from the general public and provides the city with direct information about public demand for services. It does directly confront a service-delivery establishment that is conditioned to be expansive, to seek opportunities for service. Because a price to the user greater than zero, the level implicit in tax finance, restricts use, prices are alien to government providers and charges are initially acceptable to them only as a last resort before financial crisis. They become more attractive when providers find that the new revenue flow provides them greater clout in budget deliberations because these charge-financed activities cause reduced drain on general finances.[27]

Selling services can have an adverse impact on low income people.[28] Evidence shows that receipts from the government services that many cities now sell—gas and electric, water, trash disposal, sewerage, public transportation, and hospital services—are distributed regressively against annual household income.[29] Many other services, if sold, would show a similar pattern, although data and experience are not sufficient for more than speculation. Some others—for instance, the local airport charges now encouraged by the federal government—might have much less severe regressivity. But the regressivity objection misses an important question: Why should services be provided free to identifiable affluent people in order to protect the less affluent? Greater attention needs to be directed to the reasonable design of prices and to the development of mechanisms to mitigate the burden that the charge might place on some poor people.[30]

Cities often have high concentrations of federal, state, charitable, or similarly property-tax-advantaged entities. While the city must provide to such properties the services available to other properties, it seldom will receive tax revenue from them to help defray the cost of those services. Tense negotiations about in-lieu-of-tax fees may occur, often without satisfactory conclusion. True public prices for public services provide a helpful option. If the entity wishes the service, its tax status provides no shield. Not only can the charge reduce tension, but it can also yield revenue. This influence, along with the capacity of charges to extract revenue from non-resident service customers, adds even more weight to the expectation that these revenues will become more important.

Some Special Concerns

Earmarking: Earmarking dedicates specific revenues to a particular public purpose for an indefinite period. Some observers have proposed this mechanism as a device for "showing the public what their taxes pay for" as a way to ease resistance to taxes. While earmarking may fit the mood of the public, general application of the mechanism can bring important adverse fiscal consequences.[31]

Some argue that earmarking makes government operations more businesslike, because spending is constrained to a defined revenue flow; these funds self-finance the services provided to users. But the argument requires the rare close correlation between the activity generating the revenue and the service being provided. To segregate collections from a general tax provides no market-like information about specific demand or need for the service being financed. For instance, more revenue from a local sales tax rate dedicated to a drug-abuse treatment program provides no evidence of greater demand for that particular service, compared with other services. Such collections do not provide the information that product sales volume can provide a business.

Others argue that earmarking can render a new tax or other revenue source publicly acceptable by allocating its revenue to a service with strong popular support. The public accepts the tax, because it seems to bring an attractive service that might otherwise be unavailable. But that arrangement can delude the public into false security. In a multi-function government, like a city, there is no guarantee that earmarked revenue will not substitute for other revenue that otherwise would have gone to the earmarked function. In that case, the public expectation of more or better service will not be realized, adding to suspicion and distrust of public efficiency and competence.

Earmarking breaks budget process flexibility by limiting the capacity of the government to move resources to new or changed public demands. If earmarking constrains resource response to a compelling public problem, then the option of new or higher taxes becomes more likely: it is difficult to reallocate earmarked resources away from less pressing problems. Jesse Burkhead argues: "earmarking ... represent(s) an attempt, not to introduce an improved pattern of fiscal management, but to protect and isolate the beneficiaries of specific governmental programs."[32] But the attempt may not be successful. Governments will regard funds as revenue to be distributed according to their perception of public need. If there is consensus about need, earmarking is not necessary; without that consensus, earmarking will not necessarily insulate a service in a fiscal crisis. Earmarking does complicate bookkeeping and impedes flexibility; although the strategy has some political attractiveness, it can eventually erode public confidence in government.

Exporting and Local Sharing: City revenue capacity depends both on the affluence of its own residents and on its ability to export tax burdens to nonresidents. The more of the burden of its taxes and charges a city can export to nonresidents, the higher the level of city services it can provide at a given cost to its residents. Thus, cities do consider exporting possibilities in fiscal structures, some governments giving them more attention than others.

Exporting occurs through the intergovernmental fiscal system, through taxes on nonresident individuals, and through taxes with statutory incidence (impact) on business. In the federal income tax system, some city taxes are deducted in computing taxable income (city income and property taxes for individuals filing itemized returns, and all city taxes that constitute part of cost for business returns). Payment of the deductible city tax reduces part of the city taxpayers' federal tax burden. The Tax Reform Act of 1986 reduced this exporting by ending deductibility of individual sales taxes and by reducing the marginal rates that establish the amount of deductible tax that will be saved. Furthermore, the 1990 Omnibus Budget Reconciliation Act limited itemized deductions for high-income taxpayers, further reducing the city tax exporting potential. But, at least for now, exporting through the federal tax structure remains for certain city taxes, thereby allowing higher service levels than otherwise possible at a given set cost to residents.[33]

A somewhat more direct exporting opportunity involves application of taxes or charges to non-resident individuals. Because cities trade in state, regional, and national economies that lack barriers to movement of individuals as workers, owners, or consumers, many revenue—tax or charge—transactions will involve non-residents. These revenues provide an important outlet for cost exporting. Employment-based city income taxes, by collecting tax from nonresident commuters, provide one handle. Thus, a city attracting urban commuters can export some government costs through such a tax. Sales or excise taxes on items purchased by non-residents offer another export mechanism. Prices for city services—parks and recreation, hospitals, transit and so on—sold to nonresidents similarly offer an avenue for exporting. Indeed, those charges are often more easily exported, politically and economically, than are taxes.[34] Depending on the economic mix of the city, such exporting to nonresident individuals provides an important addition to city fiscal capacity that depends on revenue options available through city adoption.

City taxes on business represent a larger avenue for exporting tax burdens. Simple logic suggests that the distinction between taxes on individuals and taxes on business would be of no practical consequence; the business tax translates completely into burdens on individuals, either as owners, suppliers, or customers. But it is an important distinction in a city environment because many individuals bearing the city business tax burden will be non-residents. Thus, the business tax—whether it be the considerable share of general sales tax collections generated from business purchases, the tax paid on business personal and real property, the tax on business gross or net income, the selective excise on business utility bills, or whatever—will be viewed as an avenue for exporting or relieving residents of part of the cost of governments. For some taxes and some cities, alternatives to the real property tax are likely to be better exporters.[35]

An opportunity to export the cost of city government seems the answer to the prayers of city leaders. Exporting attracts fiscal resources to the city, from both the suburban environs and the wider national economy. It establishes a revenue capacity greater than could be based from the affluence of city residents alone. And—an added bonus—these exported costs burden individuals who have no vote in city elections. Certainly the ability to export government costs is an attractive element of city revenue systems, and because city economic structures differ, it provides another reason for seeking revenue diversity. Allowing cities greater choices in revenue structure, an option for greater diversification, provides stronger exporting opportunities than restricting that choice.

There is, however, a critical limit to direct city tax exporting. While the non-resident bearing the burden of city taxes cannot vote in city elections, the non-resident individual or business, feeling excessively put-upon by the city, can take its business elsewhere to a jurisdiction offering a more attractive combination of taxes, charges, and services. It is that competition, along with legal constraints erected by higher governments, that limits the natural desire for cities to export government cost.

Tax Base Sharing: Another avenue for grasping resources from outside the normal fiscal limits of the city, although less common than exporting, is regional property tax base sharing. Local property taxes normally accrue on the tax base physically (or legally) within the taxing unit; only the jurisdictions overlapping the location of an electric generating plant, for instance, may tax the facility. The New Jersey Hackensack-Meadowlands program and the Minnesota Twin Cities program, adopted about two decades ago, and a small program recently adopted in the Charlottesville, Virginia, area represent the notable few exceptions.[36] In these plans, commercial and industrial property value growth—40 percent of all value growth of commercial and industrial property in a seven-county area in the Minnesota instance—is pooled for the revenue benefit of all jurisdictions. The programs are intended to reduce fiscal disparities and to minimize competition for new growth.[37]

Critics of base sharing programs argue that aggressive base sharing would, however, have an important negative impact on development in the full urban area. In many instances, the economic activity that produces truly abrupt property value growth carries distinctly undesirable impacts: electric generating plants are seldom attractive neighbors, refineries or automobile assembly plants can be noisy and smelly, and regional shopping centers bring traffic congestion and interrupt prior lifestyles. Jurisdictions in which these activities are located need revenue to manage the costs accompanying them.[38]

But managing to cover financial cost to the impacted government does not settle the argument. Many of these activities, while necessary to economic survival, fall into the "not in my backyard" (NIMBY) category. Allowing neighbors the full fiscal options associated with these tax-base-rich activities could mitigate some resistance to the facility. An Environmental Protection Agency analyst has been recently quoted as saying "perhaps we can substitute DIMBY (Dollars in My Backyard) for NIMBY."[39] Aggressive intergovernmental tax base sharing clearly would reinforce the NIMBY attitude, regardless of any other controls placed on a facility or of its environmental acceptability.

On a more philosophical level, capturing regional affluence by exporting is more consistent with city autonomy than is base sharing. Revenue diversification to export represents choice within the realm of city identity; base sharing represents surrender of some fiscal independence to a metropolitan unit. If city identity and autonomy of choice are critical elements of city futures, it is no surprise that regional base sharing has not spread beyond its few implementations.

Chapter 4

Cities, Infrastructure, and Bond Markets

City governments play an important role in providing public infrastructure, the physical capital used by individuals, businesses, and governments in economic and social life. Collapsing bridges, bursting water mains, crumbling streets, and failing sanitary sewers capture public attention. But preventing the inconvenience and danger when the infrastructure fails is not the only reason for extraordinary care in the management of city infrastructure. The evidence is accumulating that public infrastructure investment tends to increase output, private investment, and employment growth.[40] Streets and highways and water and sewer systems are particularly important enhancers of private output, and cities play important roles in capital expenditure in those areas. As **Table 8** shows, when city capital expenditure, total and construction only, is adjusted for inflation and population, such spending now is little greater than 15 years ago. Construction outlay is, indeed, lower. Data also show that these capital categories have received smaller shares of city direct expenditures (general and utility) over that period.

Unless cities take care of their infrastructure, they face critical problems. First, capital outlays today are the basis for the
capital stocks that will serve the city for years into the future.
Inaction today carries implications well beyond the year of
that inattention. Second, urban public infrastructure is easier
to create in an undeveloped area than to recreate in a built-up
area; proper maintenance in a built-up area is less costly than
rebuilding the system. To replace water mains, sewer systems, and the like in an urban area creates enormous disloca-
tion, public inconvenience, and expense. Regular upkeep and
replacement allows cities to avoid incredible extra costs. And
third, cities under fiscal pressure typically respond by con-
straining capital expenditures to protect operating expenditures (wages and salaries, supplies, etc.).[41] Despite the
importance of city capital expenditure, the record is not good
and problems seem likely to persist.

Resources for city capital expenditure may come from current
revenue, including intergovernmental aid, but major shares
ordinarily will come from debt proceeds. That is especially

Table 8. City Expenditure for Capital Outlay and Construction

| | Real Per Capita Spending (1982 = 100) | | Percent of City Direct Expenditure | |
	Capital Outlay	Construction	Capital Outlay	Construction
1972	$143.5	$113.7	19.2	15.2
1977	148.0	101.5	19.1	13.1
1982	132.4	105.2	16.8	13.4
1987	147.6	109.4	16.2	12.0

Source: U.S. Bureau of Census, *1977 Census of Governments Vol. 4 Government Finances, Number 4 Finances of Municipalities and Township Governments.* (Washington: U.S. Government Printing Office, 1979), U.S. Bureau of Census, *1987 Census of Governments Vol. 4 Government Finances, Number 4 Finances of Municipalities and Township Governments* (Washington: U.S. Government Printing Office, 1990); and U.S. Office of Management and Budget, *Budget of the United States Government, Fiscal Year 1992* (Washington: U.S. Government Printing Office, 1991).

Cities, Infrastructure, and Bond Markets

true for large projects. In their borrowing, cities are subject to many fundamental market conditions that the U.S. Treasury, private corporations, states, nonprofit organizations, consumers, and others face as they trade promises to repay in the future for resources available now. Most important, when general debt market conditions are tight and the spectrum of interest rates is high, cities will face those rates along with other borrowers. They have no charmed access that immunizes them from those market conditions. **Figure 4** demonstrates for the April 1990 to April 1991 period how the yields of 30-year U. S. Treasury bonds, 25-year municipal revenue bonds, and 20-year general obligation bonds rated A and Aa have generally followed each other. While differences between yields may increase or decrease, the yield spectrum tends to move as a single entity.

Figure 4. Average Bond Yields, April 1990 - April 1991

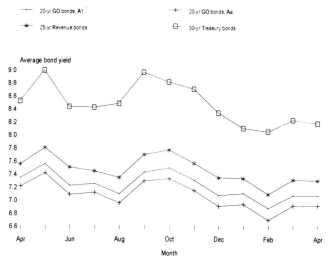

Source: "Bond Buyer Indexes," *Muniweek,* III (April 8, 1991), p. 9.

47

Cities lack the power of money creation granted the federal government by the Constitution. They can neither produce pieces of paper or metal with exchange value far above their commodity value nor, in the modern way, create checking account balances in the banking system. City debt (along with debt from other borrowers without immediate access to the U.S. Treasury) will be less secure that federal debt and each city must keep a keen eye on the willingness of the market to accept its debt. The markets constrain city debt issuance, and the markets will tell cities when their finances begin to get out of control. In this way, the powers of taxation do not distinguish cities (or other state or local governments) from private businesses in debt markets; neither has the special cushion enjoyed by the federal government.

On the other hand, cities are part of the general municipal bond market, that market for debt issued by states, cities, counties, and other special or general purpose governmental entities. Under certain circumstances, these governments may issue debt, the interest on which is not subject to regular federal income taxes. The implicit subsidy is substantial; the federal budget estimates the revenue loss from the exclusion of interest on public purpose state and local debt to be around $13.9 billion for fiscal 1992.[42] This exclusion allows such governments to borrow at interest rates below those rates that could be expected for debt of similar security and term to maturity in taxable markets. This implicit subsidy from the federal government makes regular city debt differ from that of the non-municipal market.

The Current City Debt Pattern

City government debt constitutes a relatively small portion of all government debt in the United States, around 6 percent in 1988,[43] and a considerably smaller share of the overall public and private debt market. The years of federal deficit have accumulated a debt that dominates the government sector. Cities are an integral element of the state and local fiscal system, and of that sector, the historically tax-exempt sector, city debt is a major component.

Table 9 displays the position of city debt in the overall state and local debt market. In general, cities constitute about one-fourth of total state and local debt, in total and long term. This share is somewhat greater than the one-fifth of total state and local government general and utility expenditures made by cities. The city share of debt for which all fiscal resources have been pledged for debt service (full faith and credit) is around 30 percent, as is the share of net long term debt.[44] Almost 98 percent of city debt is long term; of the long-term debt, 67.4 percent is nonguaranteed. Cities have issued about one-third of all utility debt, and utility debt makes up 22.8 percent of city long-term debt. Although cities experience occasional deficits, most borrowing finances capital asset purchase, the physical infrastructure that serves as a critical input for both public and private production of goods and services.

Debt market conditions contribute significantly to the price that cities must pay on money they borrow. But the perception of quality of that debt—the likelihood that interest and principal will be paid as due—matters as well, and this perception is reflected in the quality ratings given municipal debt by the rating firms, primarily Moody's and Standard & Poor. The difference between the top quality grade (Aaa or AAA) and the lowest investment grade (Baa or BBB) can mean differences of yield required for sale of debt of 0.5 to 1.5 percent, depending on market conditions.[45] On a multi-million dollar bond issue of twenty or thirty years term, that small difference amounts to millions of dollars of interest to be paid—and may even

Table 9. City Debt as an Element of State and Local Government Debt, 1987-1988.

Category of Debt	City Debt Share of All State and Local Debt %
Total Debt	25.1
Long Term Debt	25.0
Full Faith and Credit	28.6
Nonguaranteed Debt	23.6
Short Term Debt	28.2
Long Term Debt of Purpose	
Private Purpose	20.8
Education	4.5
Utilities	33.8
Net Long Term Debt	29.6
City Share of State and Local General and Utility Expenditure	21.2

Source: U.S. Bureau of Census, *Governmental Finances in 1987-1988*, GF-88-5 (Washington: U.S. Government Printing Office, 1990).

discourage a government from issuing the debt and making the capital investment.

Several large cities have received debt quality downratings in recent years. **Table 10** presents evidence of this debt quality problem as shown by large city general obligation ratings by Moody's.[46] For all cities with populations greater than 100,000, general obligation debt ratings are somewhat stronger—a higher percentage of cities in the top two rating classes in 1991 than in 1971, but not so many as in 1981. The same pattern appears for cities with populations above 250,000. Smaller cities show about the same share in the

Table 10. Patterns of City Credit Ratings, 1991, 1981, and 1971

	City population											
	More than 100,000 (n=181)			More than 250,000 (n=63)			100,000 to 249,000 (n-118)			Large, Older Cities (over 500K in 1950)		
Rating	1991	1981	1971	1991	1981	1971	1991	1981	1971	1991	1981	1971
Aaa	16	19	10	8	10	4	8	9	6	2	3	2
Aa	61	70	65	26	30	27	35	40	38	4	4	6
A	57	63	68	15	11	25	42	54	43	4	3	6
Baa	18	14	24	8	6	4	10	8	20	7	5	3
Ba	1	1	0	0	1	0	1	0	0	0	1	0
B	1	1	0	1	1	0	0	0	0	1	1	0
Ca	0	1	0	0	1	0	0	0	0	0	1	0
Not Rated	27	12	14	5	3	3	22	7	11	1	1	2
% Total, Aaa or Aa	42.5	49.2	41.4	54.0	63.5	49.2	36.4	41.5	37.3	31.6	36.8	42.1

Source: *Moody's Bond Record* January 1991, January 1981, January 1971.

highest grade in 1971 and in 1991, although the percentage is slightly lower in 1991. However, if the focus is on the large, older central cities, the ones which had populations above 500,000 in 1950, the quality pattern is less encouraging: the proportion of the cities in the highest rating categories has regularly declined and now stands at about one-third of the cities. Because the 1980s were generally a period of economic expansion, the deterioration of credit quality is troubling. Many cities have missed opportunities to improve their credit, sometimes through unwillingness to make difficult choices, sometimes through political disunity.[47] The decline in quality causes these cities to face higher infrastructure cost through the cost of borrowing.

Caught on the Level Playing Field

Previous sections of this book have noted the considerable interest cost advantage that cities, as well as other state and local government borrowers, enjoy because eligible debt pays interest that will be excluded from regular federal income taxes. This exclusion draws frequent analytic and Congressional attack because the exclusion reduces the progressivity of the federal income tax (recipients of tax-excluded interest are concentrated among the more affluent), costs the federal government considerable sums of revenue, and interferes with operation of capital markets by causing investment yields to differ because of tax consequences alone.

Recent federal tax revisions have narrowed the range of municipal debt eligible for interest exclusion. Industrial development bonds were early casualties. The Tax Reform Act of 1986 went further by limiting the exclusion to only certain classes of debt. The U.S. Supreme Court, in the 1988 case, *South Carolina v. Baker* (56 U.S.L.W. 4311) resolved the constitutional question "...states [and localities] have no constitutional entitlement to issue bonds paying lower interest rates than other issuers." The next major realignment of the federal income tax structure may end the tax-excluded status of new municipal debt—or at least more dramatically curtail its applicability in municipal finances.

This action will be expensive for cities, but it will not be a disaster. Cities will continue to borrow to finance capital projects. City debt will continue to be viewed as relatively secure to lenders, some city debt being seen as more secure than other city debt. Cities will borrow nationally and internationally, roughly in the same way that American corporations and the federal government do. City and other employee pension funds will even find city debt to have become a prudent investment. Cities with sound financial management, strong revenue structures, and a good economic base will have the advantage, as is the case now. But debt will be more costly.

Chapter 5

Consequences of City Fiscal Failure

What happens if a city government fails? What does it mean and what are the consequences for those dependent on city services? The dire language of city crisis used in many discussions—receivership, default, or bankruptcy—has slight relevance in the practice of municipal finance nor should they be the greatest concern of the governed. Although each would have severe consequences, all are rare.

The rarest, *receivership,* involves court appointment of an indifferent third party to preserve unit resources from likely misapplication or waste. The only known such action against a city occurred in Ecorse, Michigan in 1986. Suits by Detroit Edison, Detroit Water and Sewerage Department, and others for non-payment of bills induced the Wayne County Circuit Court to appoint a receiver with full powers for operating the government. The authority far exceeded that of any elected authority: the capacity to make dramatic changes in city services and employment, to sell city property, to contract for services formerly produced by the city, and the like—all without any political oversight. The grant of sweeping powers was never fully tested in the judicial system; the receivership ended in 1990.[48] The receivership spelled absolute loss of local control by the city government and by the people of that city.

Bankruptcy, also rare, represents an action in which a government declares itself to be insolvent and formally petitions the federal courts for assistance in debt restructuring for a realistic and orderly payment of all obligations. The municipal bankruptcy (Chapter 9 provides the reorganization vehicle for municipalities) differs radically from that of the private-sector, wherein the assets of the entity may be liquidated and proceeds used to pay creditors. The municipal bankruptcy does not envision liquidation of the offending government; creditors do not take over operations and municipal officers may retain their positions. Because state government holds ultimate authority for its localities, federal court actions in the bankruptcy must give deference to the state statutory and constitutional constraints under which the municipality operates and "the court can't interfere with municipality's political or governmental powers and its property or revenues, without the municipality's consent."[49]

Municipal bankruptcies are rare. From 1980 through early 1991, there were only 69 filings, mostly for municipal utilities; only 7 involved general governments (cities or counties).[50] Most recent city filings have been associated not with fundamental imbalance between revenues and expenditures but with major tort liabilities against small cities. They have not hinged on debt issued by the unit, with failure to pay ordinary bills and obligations, or with the normal economic fears of government, like recessions. The largest city involved, Bridgeport, Connecticut, petitioned in 1991. It sought "the court's help in rewriting its labor contracts, rather than raising taxes further and slashing public services to balance its budget."[51] The district court ruled that Bridgeport was not insolvent and threw out the case.

City *default* involves the city's failure to pay interest or principal on its debt when that payment is due. Only the lenders to the government are directly involved in the default. No disruption of services provided by the government are necessarily associated with the default nor are regular procedures or processes of the government interrupted. Officers of the city do not lose their control. Of course, any default is likely to be associated with considerable financial tensions—default does not occur lightly, first, because of negative publicity and second, because of tainted ability to borrow in the future—but the default is a borrower-lender problem on its face.

Municipal bond "[d]efault rates since the Depression have been so low that nobody even kept close track of them" until a private group, Bond Investors Association, started to do so in 1985.[52] By their tally, in 1990, the rate was 0.7 percent of around $870 billion in outstanding municipal debt, compared with 4.6 percent of corporate debt. Furthermore, municipal bond holders eventually get 50 to 60 percent of the money owed them, about 10 percentage points higher than for corporations. Evidence suggests that many municipal defaults stem from business cycle patterns.[53]

If receivership, bankruptcy, and default are not the primary concerns for failed city finances, then what is? The problem is more prosaic, less technical, and much more real. One observer captured the potential crisis especially well:

> "...the real terror of the urban fiscal crisis [is] that financially strapped cities would be unable to continue to provide those services, normally unnoticed, upon which civilized communal existence depends. The remedy...has been to cut programs and reduce employment. In the greater context of the urban crisis, however, remedies of this sort are tantamount to

embracing the ravages of a disease and calling them cures."[54]

Will cities be able to deliver the security to persons and property, the environmental management, the infrastructure and utilities, and the amenity services that the American fiscal system has assigned them the responsibility for providing? If not, then the nation will suffer, and cities will, at best, lose their autonomy and identity as their states assume control. That, not receivership, bankruptcy, or default is the result to be feared if city leaders do not meet their fiscal responsibilities.

Chapter 6

Positioning for the Future

All city governments are constrained by the economic resources available for them to tap. But some city governments will be more successful than will others. What are the elements that should help establish a sound city government fiscal status for the future?

Realism and City Leadership

Can city government leaders convince city residents that the services provided by the city are worth their cost, a cost that will be financed through city revenue sources? This will be a critical test. The 1980s were characterized by public opposition to higher taxes while voters expected at least constant and sometimes expanded public services.

Cities must prepare to deal with similar problems in the future. No enlightenment is likely to cause people and businesses to pay taxes eagerly or to demand higher taxes. But city leaders can help their position. One avenue is to ensure that city financial managers are skilled at their trade. Those skills are needed to allow city leaders to know their fiscal status and options. Without that information, leaders cannot really lead. Managers can make a difference by implementing tough fiscal decisions early, rather than by concealing problems until they become overwhelming.

City leaders can help their position by avoiding dogmatic "no new taxes" political posturing. Such a blanket assurance places an administration in a difficult position because forecasting capability does not allow certainty about all shocks that impinge on finances. It should go without saying that additional taxes (or other revenue-enhancing measures) are not popular. But an automatic rejection does not lead to responsible representative action—and it creates popular disillusionment when reality causes the pledge to be violated. Such a pledge may help win higher political office; it will not help government function.

Leaders may also improve their position by clearly communicating how the government finances its services and what services those finances provide. Traditional budget documents, with their pie charts, fund balances, and the jargon of the bureaucracy, may please the inner circle; they will not be the tools of a city leader, a person selling a vision to the population. City leaders must make a case for the value and importance of the services they provide, a case that includes the message that those services must be financed. If the case cannot be made or is not made, leaders should not blame the public—or other levels of government. The ultimate responsibility is theirs. The motto of one city's budget captures the essence of fiscal leadership: "It's not the public's job to understand the numbers. It's our job to make the numbers more understandable to the public."[55]

Revenue Diversity

Cities that are able to manage their revenue capacity will be more successful than those that feel constrained by the limits offered them by state and federal programs. Those governments best able to tap the full urban region will enjoy better fiscal success. Formal arrangements to share growth in the commercial and industrial real property base are not only unlikely but may have important disincentives for economic development to the detriment of the full urban region. Therefore, the best avenue for tapping the region would be the adoption of revenue mechanisms that permit exporting—taxes on business and commuter income, sales taxes, and charges for government service, including taxes piggybacked on state administration.

Those fiscal handles provide greater revenue diversity. Most cities will not use all these revenue sources. Their choices should be directed toward the best fiscal interests of the particular city, not toward any "ideal" standard. Each city should design a revenue portfolio for its own economic environment, revenue objectives, responsibilities, and constraints the state has offered it. No city should be automatically chastised because its revenue mix is not well-balanced among the revenue options nor because its profile is not like that of other cities. But an expanded portfolio, extending beyond heavy reliance on the traditional property tax, can help capture urban resources, prevent the tensions that emerge when any tax base carries a great fiscal responsibility, and augments the growth prospects for the revenue base. The revised portfolio would become more sensitive to national recessions and could reduce some pressure for reform of property tax administration. But those problems are less severe than the advantages from more diverse options.

Self Reliance

Cities must prepare for a more independent fiscal existence. The next major revision of the federal tax code will place at extreme jeopardy both the tax-exclusion of municipal bond interest and the deductibility of state and local income and property taxes under the federal individual income tax. The changes would end an important federal assistance historically available to cities, but both would be consistent with the drive for level playing fields and for more revenue to reduce the persistent federal deficit.

That same deficit limits the likelihood that the federal government will assume an important direct role in fiscal aid to cities or other governments. While Congress is not inclined to make tough fiscal choices to provide city governments with revenue to be spent by the cities, it is more likely to assist individuals living in cities. In other words, federal aid is more likely to flow to people rather than to places or governments; help to individuals experiencing poverty, homelessness, substance abuse, and so on, will ultimately help the places in which those people live. But large federal assistance to cities is not likely.

States have experienced recent fiscal problems, but state governments have historically shown considerable ability to respond to deficits. The long range view leaves greater hope for state assistance to cities, especially in view of the traditional position of state government as the creator of such governments. But the wise city leadership will strive for self-reliance. Not only may aid not materialize, but any aid may be for activities not fully consistent with city priorities. A substantially independent revenue structure is best suited to preserve fiscal options and governmental choices. That attitude is most consistent with city identity and autonomy in matters of importance to the citizenry.

Conclusion

Cities need to preserve their fiscal options if they are to retain individual identities and autonomy. How can city leaders best do that?

1. City leaders need to extract revenue from the entire urban area because that is, overall, where the fiscal resources of the nation and of their state are. Intra-metropolitan property base sharing is neither likely nor clearly desirable, but cities must design their own revenue portfolios to tap the full urban economic base.

2. Cities must preserve infrastructure maintenance and development in their financial plans because of the importance of the public capital stock in both private and public production. This will be difficult because debt will be more costly and because it is politically attractive to close budget gaps by deferring attention to the capital stock.

3. Cities must seek improved property tax structure and administration—even though other governments typically have responsibility for both.

4. Cities must make better use of broad sales and individual income taxes, in cooperation with their states, and make better and heavier use of charge financing. Greater attention to devices adjusting prices for low-income customers is an important element in expanding charge systems.

5. Cities must insure that other governments in urban areas have resources consistent with their public responsibilities.

6. Cities must not expect dramatic increases in federal assistance, although individual entitlements and direct agency programs may significantly help their residents.

7. City leaders must recognize that their visions of city service and finance have to be marketed to the public.

8. Finally, cities must maintain their identities and hold as much autonomy as they can. If a city becomes homogenized with its suburbs and with others of its class or, through mismanagement, becomes the ward of its state, its special contribution to the nation is diminished if not lost. Without independence, cities lose their special place in the economic, social, and cultural life of the nation.

Notes

1. Of course, the costs of living may be higher in these urban areas than elsewhere. Because federal and state revenue systems apply to absolute, not real, fiscal endowments, these measures establish where fiscal affluence will appear.

2. These data do exclude two expenditure categories: liquor stores and insurance trust (primarily employee retirement benefits). These categories, the first very small, are sufficiently insulated and specialized as to make their inclusion in the aggregate analysis improper.

3. Scott A. Bollens, "Examining the Link Between State Policy and the Creation of Local Special Districts", *State and Local Government Review* XVIII (Fall 1986), p. 123.

4. Many state constitutions assign the state the responsibility for providing "thorough and efficient" systems of public education. The problems of schools may cause major realignments in this area, for example, possibly of court intervention.

5. U.S. Bureau of Census, *Government Finances in 1987-1988,* GF-88-5. (Washington: U.S. Government Printing Office, 1990): p. 45.

6. Lawrence J. Haas, "Pleading Poverty," *National Journal* (September 165, 1990) p. 2195.

7. Direct federal aid to local governments, bypassing the state level, is not found in other federal systems. David B. Walker, "Bypassing: A Unique Feature of the American Federal System," National Academy of Public Administration Occasional Paper. Washington, D.C.: N.A.P.A., 1990.

8. Cathy L. Daicoff, "The State and Local Bond Rating Process," *Intergovernmental Perspective* XVI (Fall 1991), p. 31.

9. See Roy Bahl, *et al,* "The New Anatomy of Urban Fiscal Problems" in Marshall Kaplan and Franklin James, eds., *The Future of National Urban Policy* (Durham, N.C.: Duke University Press, 1990) for a more complete analysis.

10. David F. Sullivan, "State and Local Government Fiscal Position in 1990," *Survey of Current Business* 71 (February 1991), p. 32.

11. *Clinton v. Cedar Rapids and Missouri River Railroad,* 24 Iowa 455 (1868).

12. The "Crime of 1898" that brought Brooklyn into New York City left hard feelings in Brooklyn that still simmer.

13. Roy W. Bahl and Walter Fogt, *Fiscal Centralization and Tax Burdens: State and Regional Financing of City Services* (Cambridge, Mass.: Ballinger, 1975) and Werner Z. Hirsch, *The Economics of State and Local Government* (New York: McGraw-Hill, 1970).

14. Ted Kolderie, "The Two Different Concepts of Privatization," *Public Administration Review* XLVI (July/August 1986), p. 286.

15. Bureau of Census, *Government Finances in 1987-88,* GF-ii-5 (Washington, D.C.: U.S. Government Printing Office, 1990), p. 2, 39.

16. George W. Mitchell, "Is This Where We Came In?, *Proceedings of the Forty-ninth Annual Conference of the National Tax Association* (1956), p. 494.

17. U.S. Advisory Commission on Intergovernmental Relations, *Significant Features of Fiscal Federalism., Vol. 2: Revenue and Expenditures, 1990* (Washington, D.C.: A.C.I.R., 1990), p. 95.

18. Previous data showed them to be major providers of these functions as well.

Notes

19. Bureau of Census, *Government Finances in 1987-88,* GF-88-5 (Washington, D.C.: U.S. Government Printing Office, 1990). p.2.

20. Jens P. Jensen, *Property Taxation in the United States* (Chicago: University of Chicago Press, 1931), p. 478.

21. U.S. Bureau of the Census, *1982 Census of Governments, Taxable Property Values and Assessment-Sales Ratios* (Washington, D.C.: U.S. Government Printing Office, 1984), Table 18. "Good" means the average parcel pays property tax that is too high or too low by 10 percent or less.

22. James Heilbrun, "Who bears the Burden of the Property Tax?" in C. Lowell Harriss, ed., *The Property Tax and Local Finance: Proceedings of the Academy of Political Science* XXXV (1983), pp. 57-71.

23. States offer deferral and circuit-breaker systems to relieve this problem. But not all do and terms are often restrictive and not particularly generous.

24. John L. Mikesell, "The Cyclical Sensitivity of State and Local Taxes," *Public Budgeting and Finance* IV (Spring 1984).

25. Shawna P. Grosskopf and Marvin B. Johnson, "Land Value Tax Revenue Potentials: Methodology and Measurement" in Richard W. Lindhol and Arthur D. Lynn, Jr., eds., *Land Value Taxation* (Madison: University of Wisconsin Press, 1982), p. 63.

26. Alice Rivlin, "The Continuing Search for a Popular Tax," *American Economic Association Papers and Proceedings* 79 (May 1989), p. 115.

27. Furthermore, charges have become less expensive relative to income, property, or general sales taxes than they were before the Tax Reform Act of 1986. Lower federal rates have made use of deductible local taxes less advantageous, and the general sales tax is no longer deductible, so the taxpayer has less reasons to prefer tax to charge finance. Roy Bahl and David L. Sjoquist explore the expected effects of the new federal tax code in "The State and Local Fiscal Outlook—What Have We Learned and Where Are We Headed?," *National Tax Journal* 43 (September 1990), pp. 336-339.

28. Penelope Lemov, "User Fees, Once the Answer to City Budget Prayers, May Have Reached Their Peak," *Governing* (March 1989), pp. 24-30.

29. Robert Tannenwald, "Taking Charge: Should New England Increase its Reliance on User Charges?" *New England Economic Review* (January/February 1990), p. 64.

30. The use of special fees for low income people is not yet widespread. In a recent survey of public recreation pricing, Pagano finds lower fees for low income people infrequently at pools and golf courses and never at tennis facilities. Michael A. Pagano, "The Price of Leisure: User Fees and Recreational Facilities," International City Management Association, *The Municipal Yearbook: 1990.*

31. These comments do not apply to pledging, the dedication of a revenue source as part of a bond contract. The pledge simply insures that funds needed to service debt incurred will be provided as due; the pledge allows the debt to be sold. Neither do they apply to the pay-as-you-go budgeting principle now part of the federal budget process. This principle requires that any new spending program (or revenue reduction) must be financed either by a new revenue proposal or by reduction of an existing spending program.

32. Jesse Burkhead, *Government Budgeting* (New York: John Wiley, 1956, p. 282.

33. Early evidence does not show much state and local government response to the change in relative cost of revenue tools that the Tax Reform Act of 1986 brought. Paul N. Courant and Edward M. Gramlich, "The Impact of the Tax Reform Act of 1986 on State and Local Fiscal Behavior," in Joel Slemrod, ed., *Do Taxes Matter?* (Cambridge, Mass.: the MIT Press, 1990), pp. 241-275.

34. Tannenwald, p. 66.

35. Helen F. Ladd and John Yinger in *America's Ailing Cities* (Baltimore: Johns Hopkins University Press, 1990), pp. 50-59, find the earnings tax to be particularly powerful as an exporter, the sales tax much less powerful. Unfortunately, their estimates omit the major business purchase element in city sales taxes. Ring has estimated the business share at 41 percent, not a trivial amount. Raymond J. Ring, Jr., "The Proportion of Consumers' and Producers' Goods in the General Sales Tax," *National Tax Journal* XCIII (June 1989) im. 167-179.

36. Michael E. Bell, *Tax-Base Sharing in Maryland: A Reconsideration* (Baltimore: Johns Hopkins University Institute for Policy Studies, 1990). Ohio provides for some electric generating plant assessed value sharing.

Notes

37. Reschovsky found the Minnesota plan to be moderately successful at moderating fiscal disparities among communities but without much effect on inducing more efficient development patterns. He suggested that the program may have the long-run value of creating an awareness of economic interrelationships in the metropolitan area. Andrew Reschovsky, "An Evaluation of Metropolitan Area Tax Base Sharing," *National Tax Journal* XXXIII (March 1980), pp. 55-66.

38. William F. Fox, "An Evaluation of Metropolitan Tax Base Sharing: A Comment," *National Tax Journal* XXXIV (March 1981), pp. 275-279.

39. "Overcoming NIMBY: new Approaches to Resolving Siting Disputes," *The Public's Capital* 12 (winter 1991), p. 4.

40. Alicia H. Munnell and Leah M. Cook, "How Does Public Infrastructure Affect Regional Economic Performance?" *New England Economic Review* (September/October 1990), pp. 11-32.

41. Charles H. Levin, et al, *The Politics of Retrenchment.* (Beverly Hills: Sage, 1981.)

42. U.S. Office of Management and Budget, *Budget of the United States Government Fiscal Year 1992* (Washington, D.C.: U.S. Government Printing Office, 1991), pp. 4-36.

43. U.S. Bureau of Census, *Government Finances in 1987-1988,* GF-88-5 (Washington, D.C.: U.S. Government Printing Office, 1990.)

44. Net long term debt adjusts for debt that has been refinanced to take advantage of interest declines since the debt was initially issued.

45. Moody's Investors Service. *Moody's Municipal and Government Manual.*

46. These ratings exlcude nonguaranteed (revenue bond) debt because of the great variety of issues. However, ratings on other city issues often follow that of the city's general obligation debt. (Penelope Lemov, "Bad Times and Bad Ratings," *Governing* IV [March 1991], p. 32.) The Moody's and Standard & Poor houses do not always agree on a particular rating, but the trend is the same for each.

47. The 1990 downrating of Philadelphia debt below investment grade, despite the city's economic strength, represents a classic case of a political

clash that creates fiscal mismanagement. (Dick Kirschten, "Philadelphia Squeeze," *National Journal,* [December 22, 1990], pp. 3080-3085.)

48. Todd Sloane, "Will Ecorse Stumble Back to Its Old Course?" *City and State* (June 4, 1990).

49. Tom Herman, "What's Next In Bridgeport's Bankruptcy?" *The Wall Street Journal* (June 14, 1991), p. C1.

50. *Ibid.,* p. C13.

51. Tom Herman, "Bridgeport's Bankruptcy Petition Offers Reminder of the Plight of Cities, States," *Wall Street Journal* (June 10, 1991).

52. Lynn Asinoff and Tom Herman, "Muni Investors Study Past Defaults to Assess the Risk in Today's Issues," *Wall Street Journal.* (February 7, 1991).

53. Natalie R. Cohen, "Municipal Default Patterns: An Historical Study," *Public Budgeting and Finance* IX (Winter 1989), pp. 55-65. Many municipal defaults are of special-purpose districts, not general-purpose districts, not general-purpose governments. The Washington Public Power Supply System default in 1983 was the largest.

54. Gregory R. Weiher, "Rumors of the Demise of the Urban Crisis Are Greatly Exaggerated," *Journal of Urban Affairs* XI (1989), pp. 237-238.

55. City of Bloomington, Indiana. *Budget for Fiscal 1991-92.*

Comments

As with all papers in this series, a draft of the work of the primary author is the focus for a one-day forum in Columbus, Ohio. There, criticisms of the work are offered by a diverse group of practitioners, scholars, and observers of cities and urban government. Following the forum, with those criticisms in mind, the author is then permitted time to revise the draft for publication.

During the forum, three distinguished guests are also offered the opportunity to present comprehensive reactions to the work. For the Mikesell forum, we were fortunate to include in that panel three speakers who have written and studied extensively about the past, present, and future of state and local finance and taxation.

While the differences over Mikesell's conclusions and perspectives are marked in some of the comments, the extensions and additions to Mikesell's work made in the comments are also extremely insightful.

At the root of Mikesell's thoughts on the city of the future is a city that values its autonomy and keeps its fiscal house in order with a more diverse tax base, good management, and communications. It is a city that looks to Washington for very little and looks to its neighbors to share the cost of city services.

Given the policy hopes of urban leaders, the popular touting of regionalism, the cost and demands for urban services, and both the internal and external politics of the nation's cities, such a perspective offers much to debate, from both a prespective and descriptive view. In the three very different criticisms offered by John Petersen, Roy Bahl, and Peter Harkness that follow, much of the outline of that debate is presented.

Back to Basics

John Petersen

John Mikesell's study of city finances is thorough, thoughtful, and raises many of the right questions. While in the following commentary I take some exceptions to the scope of his diagnosis and suggested cures, the examination is a thorough one, deserving of close reading and suggestive of productive debate as to what the greatest problems are and what should be done.

That debate is timely these days because the cities that capture the popular imagination — the "national cities" that lie at the heart of regions and have traditionally been the centers of commerce, culture, transportation, and government and shape our notion of what a city is all about — are hurting and need help. It is a popular and growing perception that cities are obsolete. For many of our major cities, there is truth in that sentiment.

The decade of the 1980s, building on the transportation and population base of the previous 20 years, saw the suburban ring spring to economic and political ascendancy. Cities, in which the flagging industrial base has been increasingly replaced by communication and services, saw *those* activities increasingly pulled to the urban perimeter, as the best paid and most productive members of the work force abandoned the congestion, crime, and costs of downtown locations. City locations provide no advantage when it comes to fiber optics, faxes, personal computers, and access to airports and beltways, the tools of today's leading trades.

Cities must change, not so much to survive as to do a better job of delivering services and to remain useful in solving problems, which are really the only reasons they exist. I see city finances as increasingly and irreversibly dependent on those of other governments, and I see cities scaling down, focusing on basic services, and shedding functions that are no longer appropriate or affordable. Cities are the geographic cores of urban regions, but the power is in their perimeters. The future of city finances will be decided in the context of what they are capable of doing in concert with others, and those decisions will not be independent or autonomous.

Comparisons of Cities

The finances of cities, beyond a point and depending on context, are difficult to compare. Cities' service responsibilities vary greatly, as do the potential resources that they can tap in meeting those responsibilities. Thus, aside from the fact that cities are municipal corporations in the legal sense, the stature and significance of cities varies so greatly as to make many comparisons among them or general statements about them dubious.

For example, one can compare the purely financial operations and position of cities (Is the city government in surplus or deficit? Is it solvent or insolvent? How close to debt limits? and so forth). But it is difficult to say much about the adequacy, efficiency, or efficacy of a city's delivery of services except on a tightly defined, case-by-case basis. One needs lots of additional information about what other governments are doing (and their service responsibilities). In fiscal year 1989, the 18,977 city governments in the United States accounted for $178 billion in direct expenditures, which was a little more than one-third of all local government spending. If we take out the seven cities that had over one million population in 1980, the remaining 18,970 cities account for only 28 per cent of all local government spending.

Cities do not exist in a governmental vacuum. To appreciate how well or efficiently a city's inhabitants are being served, the local government sector must be viewed from the bottom up, with aggregation across local governments serving a population (and likely, it is necessary to calculate in state activity as well). Moreover, the delivery, in the form of direct expenditure, may be divorced from the financial sources, which may be from revenues collected by another government. Generally, because of differences in service assignments and idiosyncratic financial flows, comparisons of municipalities that extend beyond state borders are exceedingly difficult, except when looking at the most basic indicators of financial condition (and even that is starchy).

City Identity and Autonomy

My greatest problem with Mikesell's prognosis is that he sees a transcendental purpose for, and justification of, city governments. The implication is that city government uniquely provides an institutional focus for, or in some way embodies the aspirations and missions of, city residents. I think that reality is less romantic and much more harsh. In common parlance, cities are place names, and their inhabitants are only vaguely and intermittently aware of the precise jurisdiction in which they live, work, shop, or pay taxes. Legally, cities are the progeny of the state, and their boundaries are historical artifacts that have little to do (anymore) with their economic role. That role waxes and wanes and, transmuted in the prevailing political system, determines both service requirements and revenue capacity. As economic roles change, largely driven by forces far beyond a city's control, so will the demands on, and capacity of, the local economy and, correspondingly the fiscal fortunes.

Professor Mikesell argues that the greatest loss a city can experience is that of autonomy; but city autonomy is a legal construct, not an economic one. Freedom to act where there are few resources (or few service responsibilities) is substantively an empty notion. I have trouble with the personification of cities or investing them with symbolic importance. I agree that the progressive weakening of cities means a weakening of local democracy. What I am uncertain of is if, in view of the nature of the challenges facing local government, including cities, such a weakening of local autonomy is necessarily a negative for the populace being served. Local democracy is a wonderful method for solving local problems, but the problems that mean the most to the inhabitants of cities are not local, but regional and national.

Fiscal Conditions and Intergovernmental Environment

I agree with Mikesell when he cites the federal deficit as casting a long shadow over the subject of city fiscal futures. The ways in which the deficit has undermined the fiscal situation of cities are several, and I will boil these down to five that are especially significant.

First, there has been the decline in direct grants to city governments, as he documents.

Comments

Second, the decline in grants to states (and other local governments) has meant passing around the "services" hat, into
which local governments have fewer financial resources to
contribute.

Third, the federal deficit has sapped the political process and
stifled the means by which there might be federal leadership
and, correspondingly, funds to undertake new initiatives to
cure old problems. Under the tit-for-tat federal financial re-
gime institutionalized in Gramm-Rudman, the interest
groups have all been too busy preserving what they have,
meaning that no new revenues are available to undertake new
programs, a situation that kills creativity.

Fourth, the deficit has induced Congress to accomplish what
program goals it can muster by mandate and regulation
rather than by assistance, literally cascading the financial
responsibilities down the intergovernmental structure.

Fifth, the reduction in federal aid has increased competition
among governments. Jurisdictions now must use their own
fiscal resources in competing with one another for economic
activity and the jobs that go with them. Nowhere is this more
clearly evident than in the arena of economic development.
Federal aid programs to cities (such as Urban Development
Action Grants, Community Development Block Grants, and
the Economic Development Administration), had many
faults, but they did provide ammunition for development
programs that did not lean heavily on city resources. This was
particularly true of the federal tax policy that permitted the
use of the ubiquitous tax-exempt industrial development bond
and the bevy of investment-oriented tax breaks that encouraged historic rehabilitation and low-income housing, both of
which were well targeted to benefit larger, often improvident
cities. Practically all of these federally funded levers are gone,

swept away by the series of reforming tax acts of the early and mid-1980s. Cities and other local governments must fight the increasingly fierce wars of competition for jobs with their own resources. Even with state help, for many cities such resources are dwindling rapidly.

Consolidation and Reorganization

My major bone to pick with Professor Mikesell lies in the area of regionalism and governmental reorganization. He worries much about the loss of identity and autonomy. But he does not address the fact that these losses may make very good sense in a world that is changed. The altered economic function of cities, their greater exposure to events and trends beyond their control, the regional nature of major service responsibilities, and hard-nosed philosophies about what cities should do (be cost-effective, above all else) lead one to conclude that sentimentality about cities as we have known them is misplaced, at best, and detrimental to solving problems, at worst.

Governments, especially local ones, are always adjusting to meet social goals and economic needs, not vice versa. In the 1930s, there was a massive transfer of the welfare function from local governments to the states and federal governments. In the 1950s and 1960s, school districts were consolidated en masse. In the 1960s, the federal government became the major financier for constructing highways and sewer systems (although states and localities got to run and operate them once they were built). In the 1970s and 1980s, the states came to dominate financing of local schools, with the revelation that they were constitutionally and ultimately held responsible for educating children.

The major political issues of the day, traffic congestion, environmental concerns, economic well-being, are all problems with a larger compass of operational requirements and concerns than individual cities can address alone. State and regional solutions are the most likely to be implemented if there are to be any governmental responses at all in the foreseeable future.

Privatization

Professor Mikesell spends little time on privatization, believing that it cannot be viewed as a general response to fiscal stringency. As he notes, privatization is an ill-defined buzz word that suggests that greater economy and efficiency in government can come from putting more of its activities in the hands of the private sector. Greater involvement by the private sector can have advantages, quite aside from ideological considerations. Private firms can have lower labor costs, for example, because they can bypass union and civil service work rules and wage rates. Governments can put more competition into the procurement and delivery of services, especially for those services of a purely technical, as opposed to a governmental, nature. Some functions simply do not enjoy the measure of public support necessary to justify their staying in the public sector (heavily subsidized higher education, for example).

But adoption of privatization on any large significant scale or for a major functional area suffers some serious impediments. First, private firms must make a return on capital and pay taxes, costs that governments do not have. The cost of capital is higher for private companies because states and localities can borrow more cheaply by virtue of the tax-exemption of interest on their obligations and need no equity, to boot. Furthermore, private companies hired to carry on governmental activities need to be contracted with, and those contracts must be drafted, awarded, monitored, and enforced. These activities, requiring skills often not abundant in government, are themselves elements of cost for the contracting government. Finally, there are the legal problems of delegation of governmental responsibilities and the commensurate ensuing liabilities. Governments, because of their superior legal powers and, in the last analysis, greater potential financial power, are better able to deal with risk than the private sector. The image of governments as superior economic risk-takers may not be a popular one, but it is true. Besides having deeper pockets, they usually get to set the rules.

While I carry no particular brief for privatization, I am more sanguine than Mikesell about its prospects as a means of lowering costs and shedding responsibilities and thus alleviating pressure on general fund budgets. Cities, I believe, will increasingly seek out ways, through contracts, franchises, and regulations, to directly involve or indirectly steer the private sector into meeting needs that the government attempted to meet from its own resources.

City Revenue Structures

Institutionally, cities have three major problems with designing revenue systems. First, under the general strictures of the Dillon rule, city revenue structures are held hostage by the state. Second, cities seldom have exclusive reliance on a tax base. They share it with other units of local government, the states, and the federal government. Third and last, all cities are entrepreneurial in that they compete with others in terms of the quality of their services and the associated tax-price of those services.

Comments

Mikesell focuses on two aspects of the local revenue system; the property tax and user charges and fees. The property tax has its flaws, but it has virtues — great ones, in fact — if it is fairly and efficiently applied. The property tax, maligned for its plodding ways, was of course responsible for much of the recent growth and subsequent decline in local government fortunes. Through the boom of the 1980s, property tax revenues in growth areas floated effortlessly upward as property values inflated. The burgeoning of real estate under the influence of stimulative federal tax measures and easy credit made revenues roll even as tax rates were being reduced.

Recently, the whole process has reversed, with real estate values in many places (especially those of commercial properties and raw land) in steep descent. Next time, and that is likely to be many years away, greater care should be taken in not spending what is now seen as such a windfall of revenue growth on recurring budgetary items.

User charges and fees have been the strongest growth element in city revenues for some time, and while Mikesell acknowledges their fiscal fecundity, he worries about too great a reliance on them, mainly because prices are alien to government service providers. A collateral objection is with the adverse impact on the poor. Prices cannot be substituted willy-nilly for taxes, but the greater use of user charges that better reflect costs for costly, rationable, measurable services — such as water and sewer, solid waste disposal — is not only expedient politics, it is good public finance as well. The fact that charges taken in isolation may be regressive in impact is a separate question, unrelated to identifying their costs and wanting to limit their consumption. Moreover, the wisdom and ability of cities to practice home-grown redistributive policies in pricing utility types services are questionable.

City Financial Failure

Mikesell discusses in general terms the various legal forms of financial failure — receivership, bankruptcy, default. When it comes to cities and other general units of government (as opposed to limited-purpose districts), such failures as they are legally defined are rare in the extreme. More likely (and most would argue, more desirable) is that the state government will step into the breach and assume some form of oversight or control to guide the improvident or errant municipality back on the fiscally straight and narrow. Defaults on "municipal" debt are isolated among special purpose obligations, especially those that represent nongovernmental obligors (private activity obligations).

Mikesell is right in that the problem of failure is not insolvency or default but the steps that governments must take to avoid those legal forms of failure. The usual failure is a condition of chronic fiscal stringency, where an impoverished government fails to deliver on services that citizens would like to have. This can result from many causes, not the least of which are those that are self-inflicted by politicians that either mislead or fail to lead and by electorates that reward such behavior by their leaders. The political dynamic can be complex, but is usually the result of that local democratic process that Mikesell extols. On the one hand, there has been the conservative attitude (made famous by David Stockman in federal finances) that tolerates, if not actively encourages, the impoverishment of government finances as a means of reducing its size and burden. But also contributing to the current pain was the liberal attitude that good times were here to stay and the setting of overly expansive agendas based on overly optimistic revenue expectations. By hindsight, we know that the case prevailed in high-growth areas where tax revenues were spiraling. But the transgressions in the public sector pale in comparison to those in the private sector.

Infrastructure, Bond Markets, and Tax-Exemption

Mikesell stresses the importance of capital facilities to economic vitality and growth and laments the decline of the absolute and relative importance of infrastructure investments. He notes that the failure to keep infrastructure in good repair can lead to ultimately higher costs. I agree with the general contours of that argument, but I caution that it is hard to generalize on outcomes of infrastructure investment, which should be examined on a case-by-case basis. Recent economic research is suggestive of the positive role of public capital in enhancing national output, and by implication that of local areas. But infrastructure investment is a necessary, not necessarily a sufficient, condition for increased productivity. Basic market forces need to be there: Public capital investment is needed to accommodate growth forces arising from the private sector, but it will not unilaterally stimulate them. But I do agree with the author that to the degree public investment adds to productivity and supplants current consumption, it will promote economic growth.

Debt statistics regarding cities need to be treated very carefully. They need to be scrubbed for nongovernmental financing where the city or its dependent entities have acted as an intermediary or conduit and where they do not bear the ultimate responsibility to pay. Examples of nongovernmental debt includes industrial facilities, nonprofit or for-profit health care and hospital facilities, housing, and the like. Debt for governmental purposes has not grown in relationship to resources (current operating and transfer costs have grown much more rapidly). Declines in ratings on city bonds are reflections of current uncertainties about the economic base and more volatile revenue systems, not reactions to their debt burdens.

Mikesell warns that federal tax exemption of the interest on state and local bonds may soon be at stake as the federal government attempts to raise more revenues. I see this threat as remote, especially given the tight nexus between the tax-exempt bond market and infrastructure spending, a linkage made much stronger by the restrictions on tax-exempt financing put in place in the 1986 Tax Reform Act. Given other changes in the Tax Code, the lowering of the top marginal rate and the dramatic reductions in other tax preferences, the tax-exempt market is also performing more efficiently in terms of the foregone federal revenues better matching the savings in borrowing costs for state and local borrowers. There may be snips and stitches here and there, but no radical surgery that I can foresee.

Positioning For the Future

Mikesell in his conclusion supplies many suggestions as to what cities must do in the days ahead to improve their lot and that of their residents. First, there is the admonition that voters must be made to make realistic choices, that the free-riding attitude of the 1980s (for example, no new taxes are needed if we just get rid of waste, fraud, and abuse) needs to be dispelled. He's correct on that, but I think that the problem-solving process will tend to take place not so much in cities as around and through them. The biggest problems afflicting cities — traffic, jobs, land use, environmental controls and costs, welfare, the homeless — are largely beyond the ability of the city governments to solve by themselves. One reform that I believe will result from the current hardship will be more regionalism, and in many cases it will be the suburbs, politically powerful and economically more prosperous, that will call the shots.

Revenue diversification will come in the form of more regional taxes and user charge schemes, but such revenues will not likely flow to city government coffers. Rather they will go to regional entities (new and existing) that will assume functions that cities no longer can assume or that extend beyond their borders. Cities and regions will have tax systems that adhere to no theoretical standard and that vary, but the guiding principle will be to avoid individual outlier and overall burdens that increase a jurisdiction's tax prices in relationship to its competitors. And those competitors are legion, and in many cases, worldwide.

Self-reliance and an independent revenue system are the rewards for those cities that do not have too many service responsibilities (problems), are not pressed by externally ordered and unfunded mandates, enjoy relatively secure and stable local economies, and are blessed with homogeneous and affluent constituencies. These may be attributes shared by many smaller jurisdictions that have a limited menu of activities, but they are few and far between among the major cities.

Cities may strive for independence, but to an increasingly diminished and improvident player in the delivery of governmental services, that admonition is less than helpful. Many cities, not just the aged leviathans of the Northeast, need substantive help more than fiscal freedom. Their underlying economic bases are fragile and flighty, their social structures are fractured and fractious, and the costs of governance, caused by problems that transcend their outdated borders, overwhelm their resources.

Cities need not be passive in this process of change, and there is plenty they can do for themselves to alleviate problems. City management practices and political structures can often be antiquated and redundant, being more havens for entrenched bureaucracies than industrious workshops in the business of government. Budgeting, revenue administration, forecasting, and other management skills need to be improved and housed in an atmosphere that promotes professionalism. As city governments have fewer resources with which themselves to row, they will need to devote more attention to steering private-sector activities.

Solutions to the widespread mismatches of city service responsibilities and reasonably available financial resources will be met in a variety of ways. But my bet is that they will focus on slimming down city services (moving functions to other levels of government or handing them off to the private sector), and restructuring city governments to better fit with the competitive realities of the 1990s. It will be back to basics for cities, with counties, regions, and the states (themselves also pruned back) becoming increasingly the focal points of defining and financing local government services.

The Setting for City Finances in the 1990s

Roy Bahl

The prospects for financing city governments are more than
ever interwoven with the fiscal health and the fiscal attitude
of state governments. State aid, state financial assumption,
mandates and the division of revenue authority are all at the
center of any present day discussion about the fiscal position
of city governments. So, even though the focus of this forum
is cities, I have chosen to comment on the public financing
position of the state and local government sector. I think that
three issues are relevant. The first is to understand what
happened to state and local government finances in the last
decade; the second is to speculate about whether there are
some lessons that might be learned from this experience; and
the third is to identify the likely major influences that will
shape the financial health of state and local governments
during the 1990s.

What Was Different About the 1980s?

The state and local government sector stopped growing in the 1980s, as indicated by a nearly 2-point decline in the expenditure share of the gross national product. For every dollar of personal income increase in the 1970s, state and local governments spent 24 cents. This marginal rate fell to 15 cents during the 1980-1988 period. Part of the reason for this slower growth is the fiscally conservative mood of the post-Proposition 13 decade, part of it is fear that higher taxes will scare off industry, and part of it is less elastic tax structures (flatter income tax rate structures, lags in property assessment, the growth in service consumption, and the continued failure to include most services in the sales tax base).

A second trend is the decentralization of financial responsibility to the state and local government sector. Federal aid has dropped from 25 to 17 percent of total revenues, from $456 in 1980 to $381 in 1989 in real per capita terms. In addition, the value of deductibility of federal taxes has been eroded with the elimination of sales tax deductibility and the reduction in the federal marginal rates. The result of all of this is that the tax price, the proportion of each dollar of expenditures that must be financed from local sources, has increased. A higher tax price increases the accountability of state and local government officials to their constituencies, because local citizens are asked to pay for a greater proportion of each budget dollar expended.

Third, the shift toward increased dominance of state government in the state and local government financing system slowed and perhaps stopped in the 1980s. This was in part the result of passing through to local governments the cuts imposed by the federal government, and in part the result of the hesitance of states to increase taxes in order to finance higher levels of state aid. The local property tax actually increased in importance as a revenue source in the 1980s, after a long period of decline.

Fourth, state and local governments changed their revenue raising strategies, and they altered the way they allocated their resources in the 1980s. Rather than broad-based taxes, most states looked to taxes that would be targeted on only a selected set of potential payers (selective sales taxes), on beneficiary and user charges, and on magic (lotteries, amnesties, accelerated revenue payments, temporary borrowing). States seemed unwilling to make a "permanent" commitment to alter their basic financing structure. On the expenditure side, the share of the budget spent on education decreased in every state, and the absolute amount spent fell by 1.4 cents per dollar of personal income earned. The health, welfare and highways shares of total expenditures also decreased. Those expenditure categories which took an increasing share of resources were interest, judicial and corrections, and medical assistance.

Fifth, there was less emphasis on redistribution in the 1980s. Social service spending was down, state income tax structures were less progressive, and federal grants were not equalizing in their distribution across states.

To sum up, there was a shift in responsibility for financing services from the federal to the state and local government sector, and to a lesser extent from the state to the local government sector. The entire sector stopped growing in the 1980s, and it began to disinvest in social services and in general to move away from redistributive fiscal policies. As the sector has become more self-sufficient and its politicians more fiscally accountable to their constituents, there seems to have been a shift to smaller government, and to more of an economic development focus in fiscal strategy.

What Are the Lessons From the 1980s?

As the 1980s drew to a close, many states found themselves in fiscal trouble. Part of this no doubt stems from the recession of the early 1990s, but in some states, part of the problem comes from poor fiscal planning. It is arguably true that the big problems in New York, Massachusetts, California, and Virginia would have occurred to some degree even without a recession. In virtually every state in fiscal trouble, local governments have also been hurt by the combination of the recession, the cuts from the statehouse, and in some cases, fiscal mismanagement. The question I raise here is whether some of these problems could have been avoided by better fiscal planning. I suggest three lessons that might be learned from the experience of the last decade.

Lesson #1: Don't squander windfalls; they come along too infrequently. The big spender states (New York is the prime example) had a golden opportunity to use the unexpectedly strong economic growth of the 1980s to bring their public sectors into line with the rest of the country, to remove some of the debt overhang, deal with unfunded pension liability, reduce taxes, and the like. Many states, however, seemed to take the view that this economic growth was permanent and spent without consideration of how the newly expanded expenditure base would be carried when the growth stopped. A recent analysis by the Philadelphia Federal Reserve showed that those states with the highest rates of spending in the 1980s had the biggest deficit problems as the 1990s began.

Comments

Lesson #2: There is a revenue side and an expenditure side to the budget. State and local governments should undertake long-term fiscal planning — that is, revenue and expenditure forecasting. Most expenditure commitments carry long-term implications that can be foreseen. Some examples are the operations and management implications of capital spending, debt servicing, negotiated compensation rates with public employees, and compliance with federal mandates. The right question to have asked in the 1980s was the level of the tax rate that would be required to carry these expenditures into the 1990s, under varying assumptions about the performance of the economy.

Lesson #3: There is a state and a local government sector. The leadership for comprehensive fiscal planning must come at the state government level, but this does not mean that only the finances of the state government are important. State aid programs, shared expenditure responsibilities, mandates and a plethora of regulations on the local tax base tie the two sectors together in an inextricable way. Yet the crisis of 1990-1991 saw states such as Massachusetts and Connecticut try to solve part of their fiscal problems by offloading onto the local governments. The lesson is that long-term fiscal planning by state governments should include a clear vision of the role that local governments will play and how this role will be financed. In fact, many states are taking steps in this direction. Some examples are new local taxing initiatives in Arizona and South Carolina, revision of the state aid program in Wisconsin, state assumption of expenditure responsibility in New Jersey, and a revision of mandates in Florida and California.

What Do the 1990s Hold?

Good fiscal planning, the underlying theme of the above discussion, also requires some anticipation about the major events that will shape the fiscal future of a state. The next decade will be a period during which external events and federal policies will have a major impact on what state and local governments are able to do with their budgets. Here are some of the major issues I see ahead.

1. **Federal Policy:** There likely will be more of a decline in federal grants, and the value of deductibility of state and local taxes could be further eroded as the federal government continues to search for a way out of its deficit problem. This will increase the tax price of local expenditures and make it tougher for local and state officials to sell tax increases. The problem will be compounded by continued federal encroachment on state tax bases, such as excise taxes and possibly even a national sales tax.

2. **Regional Shifts:** There probably was a premature celebration in Northern newspapers about the end of the Sunbelt shift. The basic causes of the movement of the 1970s — a lower cost of doing business, access to markets, better weather — are still with us. Moreover, the global economy may make the Sunbelt states more attractive than ever. While the Sunbelt cities are still "new," their air transportation services are now better than in the 1970s, business services are well developed, housing prices and office rental rates are relatively low, and the culture and amenity packages have developed substantially. The game in the 1990s will be one of attracting new activities rather than bidding firms away from other locations. The implication is that we may be reentering a period when states will once again compete fiercely with

one another for jobs and new industry, and industrial policy considerations will dominate fiscal decisions to an even greater extent than in the past decade.

3. **Changing Population Structure:** The changing composition of the U.S. population will have important consequences for state and local government fiscal picture. On the revenue side, there will be a slower growth in the working-age population. This also means that there will be fewer family-forming people, those who purchase the big ticket consumer items. The growing retirement-age population will also force reconsideration of some revenue issues, including the proper tax treatment of retirement income, and property tax relief that is age-tested rather than means-tested. Also, revenue decisions will be increasingly influenced by older Americans, who may be less sympathetic to a larger government sector. On the expenditure side, there will be an increase in the number of elderly, implying a demand for a different package of public services. By the end of the decade the school-age population will be on the decline. There is every prospect that expenditures for crime and corrections will be heavy. The 1990s will be a period of substantial adjustment (and perhaps costly adjustment) in state and local government budgets.

4. **Changing Economic Structure:** The structure of jobs and income is changing in all states, and tax systems will have to catch up. Most states have traditional tax structures that focus on commodity consumption, earned personal income, incorporated companies, and real property. But income in the 1990s is going to be heavily derived from capital sources and transfer payments, consumption is heavily in services, partnerships play a major role in service production, and much wealth is held in the form

of intangibles. State tax structures are going to have to look to these new bases if they are to produce adequate revenues and distribute the tax burden equitably.

5. **The Poor:** The 1990s will be a decade when state and local government will begin to reinvest in the poor. The problems, and their costs to society, are staggering: drug abuse, crime, teenage pregnancy, high school dropouts, black male unemployment, low birth weight, homelessness, and welfare dependency are among the ignored problems of the 1980s. State and local governments will come up against a big fiscal ticket during the next decade when they attempt to face up to these problems.

Cities on Their Own

Peter A. Harkness

I was intrigued by Dr. Mikesell's paper. In quiet, academic
prose it came to important conclusions that I think are correct.
If I had to put a headline on it, as journalists always want to
do, it would be much like the one our magazine ran atop a
recent article on the future of municipalities: "Cities On Their
Own."

What surprised me most about that article was not its conclusions, but the strong reaction they evoked from the National
League of Cities, the U.S. Conference of Mayors, and some city
officials, as well.

They might be similarly upset with Mikesell's paper, specifi-
cally because he concludes that the direct link between the
federal government and the city governments is severed.

While cities can expect aid to individuals to continue, assistance to the governments themselves has dwindled and will
continue to do so. His point is correct, though I am not even
as sanguine about aid to individuals.

The reason is the federal deficit, and on this subject I may
have a somewhat different view than Mikesell. His paper
notes that because of politicians' "fears" concerning budget

deficits, there have been a series of "federal deficit control laws, each intended to be so Draconian as to induce deficit restraint and eventual budget balance."

The tone of this observation is somewhat less alarmist than my own. The federal budget is out of political control. We probably will run a deficit between $350 billion and $400 billion this fiscal year, and though an economic recovery should help cut it in the future, I'm confident it will not be reduced to acceptable levels anytime soon without much more severe spending cuts than the "Draconian" measures we have seen to date.

This year interest payments on the national debt will pass defense as the single largest item in the federal budget. The deficit we roll up this year alone will add another $20 billion to $25 billion in interest to next year's operating budget. Yet not only is there no political will to solve the problem, there is sentiment to exacerbate it further. It may well be that the political parties attempt to outdo one another yet again in a tax-cutting bidding war for 1992 election votes.

In the end, I think all federal aid to localities is jeopardized, whether it be through grant programs or income security payments to individuals. What I did not consider is that a deficit deal might prompt changes affecting state and local governments on the revenue side. Mikesell states unequivocally that "the next major revision of the federal tax code will place at extreme jeopardy both the tax-exclusion of municipal bond interest and the deductibility of state and local income and property taxes under the federal individual income tax." That's something of a stunner, and my first reaction was outright disagreement on grounds that there is no real interest in that either in Congress in general or on the two tax-writing committees in particular. But that may be irrelevant.

Comments

If there ever is to be a budget agreement that seriously addresses the deficit, this is exactly the kind of restructuring that will have to take place. It was close on the state and local tax deductibility question less than a decade ago, so there is no reason it can't happen again. Certainly, one important lesson we have learned watching the state and local lobby in Washington is that it is weak, uncoordinated, and — at least in the case of the associations representing local governments — often behind the trend of events.

I agree that cities must turn their attention to their states and away from Washington, as Mikesell advises. That is not the sentiment at the National League of Cities and the U.S. Conference of Mayors, and the advice does ring a bit hollow in the wake of the massive budget-cutting that has taken place across the state capitols in mid-1991, much of it done on the locals' backs. But it is still correct. Cities must reestablish relations with their states.

Mikesell's paper is on municipal taxation and finance, so he rightly sticks to revenues and rarely mentions spending. But it's worth noting the significant contrasts one sees in cities across the country. While an Oceanside, California, or a Naples, Florida, must cope with rampant growth, a Louisville, Kentucky, or Denver, Colorado, or Akron, Ohio, must try to stabilize a shaky economy.

New York, Boston, Washington, Philadelphia, Atlanta, Chicago, Los Angeles, and other older, larger cities are in a category unto themselves. Their experiences are important because they help form the view that many Americans have of cities. And, increasingly it is apparent that the news about the quality of governance of these urban centers is not good.

Urban leaders are vulnerable to charges of mismanagement, bloated payrolls, excessive administrative costs, and so on. The fault may not lie in their own administrations, but in the system they inherited. Sharon Pratt Dixon in Washington is having terrible trouble making the smallest cuts in a bureaucracy that is far too large by anyone's standard. In New York City, David Dinkins has the same problem.

As population counts in cities or school districts have fallen, administrative costs have soared. Newspapers in a number of larger municipalities are on to the story. Voters everywhere ascribe importance to it, and the political resistance to new taxes of any kind stiffens. Local government leaders increasingly complain that voters will only accept higher taxes when the money is earmarked for specific programs or projects, thereby reducing the flexibility officials have in administering their cities, as Mikesell points out.

The paper admonishes city officials to "improve their position by clear communication of how the government finances its services and what services those finances provide." Agreed.

But if the administration of a school system has 250 percent more employees than it did 30 years ago and student enrollment has fallen by 20 percent, then you have some hard explaining to do. Many mayors find themselves in such situations today, and it leaves them vulnerable.

And then there are mandates. As former Gov. Jim Thompson of Illinois described the President's new transportation policy last year, it was translated: "Read my lips, raise your taxes!" It's easy for politicians at one level to vote for improved or new services and order politicians at another level to pay the bill. Since local governments are at the end of the line, with declining political clout, they are the losers. I sense that this syndrome has reached a critical point where local governments are increasingly likely to "just say no." There are already cases where local governments in Maine and elsewhere have told the Environmental Protection Agency that they cannot meet deadlines because of lack of funds. And if EPA doesn't like it, they'll just have to sue. They haven't, and I'm guessing that they won't.

Finally—and it's related—there is the question of our own political behavior related to the whole question of what government can and should do.

Mikesell implores city leaders to avoid the "dogmatic 'no new taxes' political posturing." I'm afraid that's like asking the dog to stop barking. Allowing the electorate to think we can keep on avoiding hard choices has become the easiest path to electoral success. Many politicians have duped the voters, and the voters have duped themselves. It's happening at all levels of government, and, if anything, it was more widespread in the 1990 election than ever before among candidates of both parties, particularly for governorships.

Now one hears local leaders complain that citizens want more government services but don't want to pay for them. That's not so surprising considering the political rhetoric they have been subjected to for the past number of years.

The sooner political leaders are straight with their constituents about hard choices that must be made and honest with themselves about the quality of the governments they lead, the better chance they will have of achieving the most important goal Mikesell sets for them — maintaining their autonomy and identity.

Biographical Notes

John L. Mikesell is a Professor of Economics at the School of Public and Environmental Affairs at Indiana University. Mikesell received both his Ph.D. and M.A. degrees in Economics from the University of Illinois. Mikesell is involved with many public finance journals and serves as Co-editor of *Public Budgeting and Finance.*

Considered a leading authority on state and local government finance, Mikesell has written four books and dozens of articles on a broad range of public finance issues.

John Petersen is President of Government Finance Group, Inc., Arlington, Va.

Roy Bahl is Professor of Economics and Director, Policy Research Center, College of Business Administration, Georgia State University.

Peter A. Harkness is the editor and publisher of Governing Magazine.

Comments

The series editors are Dr. Michael A. Pagano, Professor of Political Science, Miami University, and John K. Mahoney, Assistant to the Director, Ohio Municipal League.

City Finances, City Futures